PUFFIN BOOKS
MISSION INDIA
A VISION FOR INDIAN YOUTH

Avul Pakir Jainulabdeen Abdul Kalam, born 15 October 1931, is one of India's most distinguished scientists. He was responsible for the development of India's first satellite launch vehicle, the SLV-3, for the development and operationalization of strategic missiles and their weaponization, and for building indigenous capability in critical technologies. As Chairman of the Technology Information, Forecasting and Assessment Council (TIFAC), he guided a number of technology projects and missions to take India into the twenty-first century. The TIFAC's document on Technology Vision 2020 is a blueprint to make India a developed country. A.P.J. Abdul Kalam held various positions in Indian Space Research Organization (ISRO) and Defence Research and Development Organization (DRDO) and became Principal Scientific Adviser to the Government of India. He has the unique honour of receiving honorary doctorates from thirty universities and the country's three highest civilian honours—Padma Bhushan (1981), Padma Vibhushan (1990) and Bharat Ratna (1997). He was Professor of Technology and Societal Transformation at Anna University, Chennai when he was elected President of India in July 2002. He has met more than 4,00,000 children all over the country to share his vision of India.

*

Yagnaswami Sundara Rajan, born in 1943, is the Principal Adviser, Confederation of Indian Industry (CII), and Adjunct Professor, BITS, Pilani. He was earlier Scientific Adviser to Punjab chief minister. He was associated with the ISRO and subsequently to the communication satellite programme, the remote sensing programme, and satellite meteorology and mapping systems.

Mission India

A Vision for Indian Youth

A.P.J. Abdul Kalam
with
Y.S. Rajan

PUFFIN BOOKS

PUFFIN

Published by the Penguin Group

Penguin Books India Pvt. Ltd, 11 Community Centre, Panchsheel Park, New Delhi 110 017, India

Penguin Group (USA) Inc., 375 Hudson Street, New York, New York 10014, USA

Penguin Group (Canada), 10 Alcorn Avenue, Toronto, Ontario, Canada M4V 3B2 (a division of Pearson Penguin Canada Inc.)

Penguin Books Ltd, 80 Strand, London WC2R 0RL, England

Penguin Ireland, 25 St. Stephen's Green, Dublin 2, Ireland (a division of Penguin Books Ltd)

Penguin Group (Australia), 250 Camberwell Road, Camberwell, Victoria 3124, Australia (a division of Pearson Australia Group Pty Ltd)

Penguin Group (NZ), cnr Airborne and Rosedale Roads, Albany, Auckland 1310, New Zealand (a division of Pearson New Zealand Ltd)

Penguin Group (South Africa) (Pty) Ltd, 24 Sturdee Avenue, Rosebank, Johannesburg 2196, South Africa

Penguin Books Ltd, Registered Offices: 80 Strand, London WC2R 0RL, England

First published in Puffin by Penguin Books India 2005

10 9 8 7 6 5 4 3 2

Typeset in Sabon by Mantra Virtual Services, New Delhi
Printed at Baba Barkhanath Printers, New Delhi

Contents

Preface

In the recent Indian history, very rarely have we come across a situation like that which exists now. We have an ascending economic trajectory, continuously rising foreign exchange reserves and global recognition of our technological competence. We also have the energy of 540 million youth, the connectivity of 20 million people of Indian origin in various parts of the planet, and the interest shown by many developed countries to invest in our engineers, scientists and other professionals including setting up of new research and development centres in India. The government is committed to economic development by ensuring a growth rate of 7 to 8 per cent annually, enhancing the welfare of the farmers and workers, and unleashing the creativity of the entrepreneurs, businesspersons, scientists, engineers and other productive forces of the society.

Our book *India 2020: A Vision for the New Millennium* is all the more important now, when the youth has tremendous opportunities to work in various important knowledge sectors like agriculture, industry, and information and communication technology.

When *India 2020* was published in 1998, the original English edition became a best-seller, as did the Tamil edition. These two editions have together sold more than 2,20,000 copies. The book has subsequently been translated into nine other Indian languages, as well as Chinese, Serbian, Croatian and Sinhalese.

I have received hundreds of letters and emails from people

saying that this book gave them a mission and the boldness to act. People from all walks of life use it as reference material. Institutions have taken inspiration to start small- and large-scale industries. This book has become part of syllabus in some universities and schools. Other authors and editors have quoted from it extensively.

This students' edition, *Mission India*, is intended primarily as a road map for young people. It will also be useful for young entrepreneurs. The facts, figures and tables have largely been taken from *India 2020*, but have been updated and modified to suit the new readership.

The book begins with the poignant question: can India become a developed country? The chapter analyses our strengths and weaknesses, and concludes that we should have faith in ourselves and give our undivided attention to the goal of making India a developed nation.

The next five chapters look at five core industries where we must acquire a reasonable self-sufficiency over the next decade and half in order to achieve this goal. These are agriculture and food processing; materials and the future; chemical industries and biotechnology; manufacturing for the future; and strategic industries. There is a lot more that can be done to develop these industries and each chapter looks at what we must aim for each area.

The seventh chapter discusses the services sector and the Indian education system. It emphasizes the need for inputs relating to research and inquiry, creativity and entrepreneurship in our educational system to make a attitudinal change in the young minds, and looks at the latest technology tools that can be used to take quality education to all corners of the country.

The eighth and ninth chapters, 'Healthcare for All' and 'The Enabling Infrastructure' deal with two aspects which are the sine qua non of a developed nation. These chapters look at the present conditions in these vital areas and analyse what has to be done to achieve a new dimension. Also given are examples of the role played by emerging technologies in these vital sectors.

The last chapter, 'Realizing the Vision', takes a final look at the trends seen in India's development today. It outlines how every individual and organization can play a role in reaching our goal. This chapter, we believe, is crucial for everybody to decide on what she/he can do for this great mission of transforming India into a developed nation.

I would like to dedicate this book to all those Indians who believe that we can achieve the goal of Developed India Vision 2020.

My greetings and best wishes to you all.

February 2005   A.P.J. Abdul Kalam

Can India Become a Developed Country?

In the days before Independence, India had many dreamers; many capable men and women who dreamt of a strong and modern India. They realized that to be strong and modern, India needed to develop in many and diverse areas. You must have heard of many of them: Mahatma Gandhi, Jawaharlal Nehru, Sardar Patel, Maulana Azad, Subhash Chandra Bose, Bhagat Singh, Sarojini Naidu, Rabindranath Tagore, C.V. Raman and J.N. Tata. The lives of these men and women and many others, many of whom were at the forefront of the Independence movement, make for wonderful reading, as they inspired a new generation of leaders. They worked in many different fields: political, social, economical and literary; but with one single goal: to free the nation from slavery and give it its due place in the world.

After 1947, India was inspired by the shining examples of these men and women. Great progress was made in many aspects of national life—agriculture, industry, health, education, roads, railways and other fields. India's vibrant democracy—despite the huge population with the associated problems of illiteracy and poverty—was a wonder to the world.

India started major efforts to develop in the fields of science, technology and industrialization, with considerable amount of foreign collaboration. We wanted to speed up the rate of industrialization in the country as western nations had been leading in this field for over 250 years. Some of the new Indian industries did well but many were excessively reliant on foreign technology and repeated re-imports.

As a result, many vital sectors began to depend on foreign sources for innovation or technology. Though government policy stated that self-reliance and commitment to science and technology were India's goals, in practice, however, things were often different.

Let us look at the example of one of the most crucial materials—steel. As you know, steel is made from iron. Steel is essential for every kind of construction—buildings, bridges, railway tracks, ships—and therefore vital for a new nation which was striving to be industrially and technologically developed. The visionary industrialist J.N. Tata had realized the importance of steel and built a steel plant at Jamshedpur many years before Independence. Otherwise steel production in India was very low, though we have some of the best iron ores. To give the steel industry a head start, India sought help from three countries. The former Soviet Union (now broken up into many republics) helped in setting up plants at Bhilai and Bokaro in the mid-1950s and 1960s. Britain aided India in building the plant at Durgapur, and West Germany for the plant at Rourkela. But instead of adapting the foreign technology to our needs, and innovating on the knowledge to build better future plants with Indian design, India remained dependent on foreign assistance for the steel sector for many decades. The story was similar in several other sectors.

Why is India poorer than some other countries?

You may wonder why there is so much abundance in some countries, and poverty and deprivation in others such as India. Why is it that these countries were in a position to help us?

There is nothing mysterious about this. The historic fact

is that people of these 'developed' nations believed for many years that they must live a good life in a strong and prosperous nation. They were ready to work hard for achieving their goal. They took risks. With great discipline, focus on their goal, and a strong work ethic, they worked so that their reality became aligned with their dreams. With a similarly strong sense of purpose, we too can achieve a good life for all people in India.

The *Thirukkural*, an ancient Tamil poem which I love, says:

வெள்ளத் தனைய மலர்நீட்டம் மாந்தர்தம்
உள்ளத் தனைய துயர்வு

(Whatever the depth of the river or lake, and whatever the condition of the water, the water lily always blossoms.)

Similarly, if there is determination to achieve a goal, man will always succeed.

This determination to achieve a goal can work wonders. During World War II, Japan was virtually destroyed. Fifty-four Japanese cities were bombed and Tokyo reduced to rubble. Three million Japanese were killed and thousands more died later of malnutrition. Until 1949, the economy was in deep trouble. Yet today, Japan is one of richest countries in the world. This was achieved, among other things, by the sheer determination of the Japanese government and people. Similar is the story with South Korea, whose industries are dominating many world markets.

The greatest danger to our achieving our goal comes from our own lack of confidence in our abilities. This danger is further increased when we allow ourselves to be distracted from our purpose of developing the country by those who seek to divide the people and spoil our sense of being one united nation in quest of a common goal. The Indian

Constitution bestows equality on all citizens. The time has long come for us to stop differentiating between people of different religions, castes and lifestyle choices. India's beauty lies in its diversity and freedom. Let us rejoice in these qualities, and use these as positive assets as we work with determination and discipline to make all of us prosperous. It is only when we accept all Indians in all their magnificent and delightful diversity that we can look forward to a shared future of peace and prosperity, of creation and abundance. We must learn from our common past, but it is the future we have to build—and we can only do it if we see ourselves as one nation with a common goal.

India's heart has always lain in its villages—70 per cent of our people live there. It is to these villages that we must go back if we are to truly develop. Indian villages can no longer be poor and lacking facilities. They are to be transformed with the modern knowledge. The developed India will be a network of prosperous villages empowered by various connectivities: physical as well as virtual, telemedicine, tele-education and e-commerce. Developments in biotechnology, biosciences, agricultural sciences and industries will aid the emergence of the prosperous new India. Helping the process will be political leaders and administrators who will devote themselves with a professional attitude to their work, disregarding individual interests and political influences. This attitude will lead to minimizing the rural–urban divide. Modern lifestyles will become available to the rural people also. At the same time, the natural beauty of the countryside must be carefully protected.

What is a developed country?

When we talk of a developed country, it has many aspects to it. The indicators are the wealth of the nation, the prosperity of each of its people, and its standing among other nations in international forums. But in practice, you don't need detailed facts and figures to work out which countries are 'developed'. You can see the difference between a developed country and developing country if you simply look around you.

In a developed country, there are certain facilities which one takes for granted as an essential part of living. For example, there are good roads, street lighting, no garbage on the streets, water whenever you turn on the taps. Are all these things true when you look around?

Being 'developed' does not mean that people in those countries can sit back and do nothing. Hard work is a part of life. What it means is that there are various facilities which they take for granted, which we, in India, cannot. For example, there are educational facilities for all, distributed all over the country. There is a constant supply of electricity, so that the power does not go off just when you are studying for an exam the next day. When you go to a hospital, there are enough doctors and the hospitals are clean and well equipped. When we find all these things in every part of India, only then can we call ourselves truly developed.

The wealth of a nation

The term used to indicate creation of wealth of a nation is **gross domestic product** (GDP).

> **GDP** is the sum total of all goods, services, and other moneys earned by the country in a given year. It includes all the money spent on goods for consumption and on investment by each individual and companies, as well as government expenditure, and the total value of exports over and above the money spent on imports.

To compare the GDP of different countries, we convert all the sums of money into one unit—usually the dollar. You know that different currencies have what is known as an exchange rate, which is the price at which you can buy or sell that currency with your own domestic currency. The exchange rate of the rupee and the dollar right now is about Rs 45 = $1. However, you cannot buy for $1 the same things as you can afford to buy for Rs 45. A man who earns a salary of $1000 a month in the US is not a rich man, but a man who earns a salary of Rs 45,000 a month in India is a rich man.

This is where a new concept comes in, which is **purchasing power parity** (PPP).

PPP is a method used to calculate exchange rates between the currencies of different countries. PPP exchange rates are used in international comparisons of standard of living. They calculate the relative value of currencies based on what those currencies will buy in their nation of origin. Typically, the prices of many goods will be considered, and weighted according to their importance in the economy.

Countries with highest GDP in the world in PPP terms (2002)

Country	GDP
USA	10.40
China	5.70
Japan	3.55
India	2.66
Germany	2.18
France	1.54
UK	1.52
Italy	1.44
Russia	1.35

All figures in US $ trillion

The US is first in the list, and India is fourth. We are not doing too badly, you might be saying. But let us take a closer look at the differences between India and the US:

	USA	India
Land area	93,72,610 sq km	32,87,590 sq km
Population	282 million	1016 million
2002 GDP ($ trillion)	10.40	2.66
Per capita income (PPP)	$36,300	$2,900
Literacy	97%	62%
Life expectancy	Male 73; Female 79	Male 63; Female 61.4

The per capita income in the US is almost thirteen times that of India. Naturally our prosperity is much lower.

Per capita income means total income (GDP) divided by the number of people.

The prosperity of the people

India has to support its huge and growing population. Therefore, we need to create more wealth to improve the standard of life for our people. That means our economy has to grow fast. The US economy grows at an average rate of 2.5 per cent. Our GDP has to grow at a much faster rate of, say, 10 per cent per annum. Only then can we remove poverty and become a prosperous developed country soon.

Economic indicators are important but they provide only part of the picture. The numbers can hide a lot of human misery.

Per capita income does not indicate the differences which exist in wealth. You know from looking around you that not all the people have the same amount of money. The woman who comes to clean your house does not earn the same amount as your parents do. It is unlikely that your parents earn as much as a big industrialist does. Yet when per capita income is calculated, these differences in income are not shown by the average figures.

It is true that such disparities in income exist all over the world. But in a developed country, even the people earning at the lower income levels are able to have a better life due to the availability of certain facilities, which do not exist in developing countries. There are many social security schemes which can help people during difficult periods of unemployment or prolonged sickness. Increased use of technology ensures that people do not have to struggle with low-skill and low-pay jobs such as that of a rickshaw-puller or a servant.

> The National Sample Survey 1999–2000 indicates that 23–26 per cent of the Indian population, or 236–264 million people, are below the poverty line. This represents a significant reduction from the previous estimate of 36 per cent, or 323 million people, in 1993–94. We need to make it 0 per cent by 2020!

A reasonable lifespan, an occupation which can provide everyone with basic comforts and good healthcare are the essentials for everyone in our dream of a developed India. To assess how well a country provides these things for its citizens, there are certain questions we must ask:

1. Do all people have adequate and nutritious food?
2. How long does the average person expect to live?
3. How many infants survive their early years?
4. Is there drinking water available, and is it of good quality?
5. Is there reasonable sanitation and good environment in a person's home and place of work?
6. Are there good medical facilities available?
7. Are there good educational facilities available, which offer

students choices so that they can follow their interests?
8. Are people able to acquire the skills needed to get jobs that pay well in the modern world?
9. Are there good infrastructures such as roads, uninterrupted and adequate electric power and telecommunication?
10. Do people generally feel safe?

It is only when all these are available to every person in the country that we can say the nation is truly developed.

Standing in international forums

In olden times, a country's standing in the world was determined by the area of its conquests and territories. Nowadays, a country's standing is determined mainly by its economic power.

As communications improve, the world has become one big marketplace. If you live in a big city, you can probably find apples from the US or kiwi fruit from New Zealand for sale at your local market. This flow of goods from the country of origin to markets in other countries is part of the phenomenon known as globalization.

The free flow of goods and services happens within the country all the time. Thus, people in Punjab would buy apples grown in Himachal and medicines made in Maharashtra—because these areas are major centres for producing these things. But at the same time, because Punjab is a major grower of wheat, people in Himachal and Maharashtra would buy wheat grown in Punjab.

In theory, globalization means that this unfettered flow of goods and services happens not just within all regions of a country, but between all countries in the world. So a country which could produce cars cheaper and better than others would sell cars to other countries, which could not produce them that cheaply. At the same time, if the car-producing country could not produce computers that cheap, it would buy computers from another country which could produce them at lower cost. This is also described as making the best of comparative advantages that a country possesses.

> **Globalization** can be described as when countries produce goods and compete with other countries to sell them worldwide. It leads to growth in international trade, investment and capital flows, and results in economic growth for who are economically and technologically efficient.

What makes countries decide what to produce? It could be natural advantages, such as the geography or the climate or the availability of natural resources. It could also be that a country has a long tradition of specialization in the production of that particular good or service, such as wine in France. An area in which a country has certain advantage or ability to produce is known as its core competency.

> A **core competency** is fundamental knowledge, ability or expertise in a specific subject area or skill set.

Thus, the idea behind globalization is that all nations will develop their core competencies and manufacture or do things which they are best at doing. Such competition, both within the country and with other global players, would be useful to make the country efficient and strong.

In practice, however, there are often barriers to the flow of goods and services. As every country is trying to sell to the same global marketplace, it is natural that those with more influence will try to make things easier for themselves. Some developed countries deny opportunities to other countries to reach a developed status. Even when one prepares to cope with a set of barriers introduced by these developed countries, a new set crops up. India has to be prepared to face such actions by more powerful countries as it tries to march ahead to realize its vision.

The way forward

In order to achieve a developed India, it is essential that we believe in ourselves, and we believe in what we as a nation can do.

Somewhere along the line, we seem to have lost faith in ourselves. We seem to have a blind faith in things done beyond our borders. Many people think that things are better simply because they are foreign. See for yourself—when you go into a shop, even a grocery shop, people often buy foreign products. Shopkeepers say something is foreign-made as a badge of quality. Buyers are willing to buy even shoddy imported goods in the belief that they will in some obscure way be better than what is being manufactured in our own country.

Sometimes we find it hard to give India credit for its achievements. I have a glossy, superbly produced German calendar with maps of Europe and Africa based on pictures taken from satellites. When people are told that the satellite which took the pictures was the Indian Remote-Sensing (IRS) Satellite, they are occasionally disbelieving. They have to be shown the credit line under the picture.

As a country, we have to be bold and set a course for ourselves. When Gandhiji adopted ahimsa and satyagraha as methods of obtaining freedom, it was a great innovation. Today, too, we have to make great innovations and chart our own way to the India of our dreams. The most important task before the country's leaders is to bring together all the people who can change the country and make them work towards this goal together and with great urgency. And each and every Indian can make a difference, especially the nation's youth.

Detailed studies show that the main planks of India's development are:

Agriculture and food processing	Healthcare
Materials and manufacturing industries	Education
Chemical industries and biotechnology	Critical technologies
The services sector	

Within each of these areas, India has certain core competencies, which need to be developed to achieve full utilization of the potential. In this book, you can read about what India has achieved in these areas, and what India needs to achieve in order to reach our goal of being a developed nation by 2020. Read it, understand our country, and see what you can contribute to realizing Vision 2020.

Agriculture and Food Processing

When I think of India, I think of endless green fields of wheat, rice, other crops and vegetables, of a gentle river winding its way slowly, and of green trees around shady village ponds. India is a fertile country with lots of natural resources. We can certainly produce enough food to feed our billion-strong population, especially with the Second Revolution.

One of the reasons why growing enough food is important is because food output has to match the growing population.

Year	Population (in millions)
1700	127
1900	271
1947	345
1960-61	439
1970-71	548
1980-81	683
1990-91	846
1999	1,000
2000-01	1,027

You will notice that since Independence the increase in population has been rapid. Thus, however much food we produce, it is very hard to match the rate at which our population is growing. But with modern methods there can be solutions to this problem, when one brings together India's rich land farmed by enterprising farmers and the excellent agricultural technological know-how now available.

You are too young to know about the acute food shortages in the 1960s, when there was a long drought, and India was greatly reliant on wheat imported from the US. The late C. Subramaniam, who provided the thrust for the Green Revolution from the political side, while agricultural scientist Dr M.S. Swaminathan handled the technological part, describes the crisis that took place in India in the mid-1960s thus: 'During ... that critical period of drought [1966–67], President Johnson, because of certain policies he had adopted, was releasing wheat only in driblets. At one point, we reached a stage where there were stocks for only two weeks and nothing else in the pipeline.'

This crisis situation made the country's leadership resolve to use our strengths to remove the dependence and become self-sufficient in food grains. This effort was known as the Green Revolution.

The Green Revolution

The Green Revolution was launched to liberate India from what was called 'ship to mouth existence'. During the period 1967 to 1978, there were three major changes made to the traditional agriculture practised in India. More land was brought under irrigation, double-cropping was introduced on existing farming land, and most importantly, new, high-yielding varieties of seeds were used along with fertilizers. These changes were supplemented by institutional support to the farmers in terms of marketing their produce. As a result of this effort, India achieved food grain sufficiency in the 1970s, with a record 131 million tons of food grains produced in 1978–79.

As you can see from the table that follows, as a result of

the Green Revolution, India's food grain production has grown dramatically. The need to import food grains is now minimal, and there are adequate buffer stocks. In June 2002, buffer stocks stood at 64 million tons. We can now even export certain quantities of food grains. When two of the worst droughts occurred in 1979 and 1987, there was no need to ask anyone for food aid.

	1950	1960	1970	1980	1990	2000
Food grain production	50.8	82.0	108.4	129.6	176.4	201.8
Food grain import	4.8	10.4	7.5	0.8	0.3	-
Buffer stock	-	2.0	-	15.5	20.8	40.0

All figures in million tons

If all Indians have to have good nutrition and plenty of food, then we need 360 million tons of food grains by 2020. This will allow for good domestic consumption and still leave a sufficient margin for food exports and aid to other countries in need. This mission will demand a great revolution in research, technology development, agricultural extension services and, above all, a major network of marketing, storage and distribution. There are other challenges ahead. We are still heavily dependent on the rains. If there is a succession of bad years, output gets affected. To resolve all these remaining problems, we require a Second Green Revolution.

The Second Green Revolution

According to C. Subramaniam, with whom I once discussed this issue, India has to embark upon the Second Green Revolution which will enable it to further increase its productivity in the agricultural sector. This revolution focuses on matching soil to seed, and product to market. Key parameters are high productivity and better value addition by agro-processing.

C. Subramaniam told me that his last dream was to bring about the Second Green Revolution. To this end, he had set up the National Agro Foundation with help from the Technology Information, Forecasting and Assessment Council (TIFAC).

Some of the important issues that we have to look at during the Second Green Revolution are:

Better use of resources: Productivity of land needs to be increased to feed the rising population. The poorer land can be utilized for building roads, agro-processing industries and storage facilities, all of which are needed for processing and selling farming produce. The situation is similar with use of water. A lot of present-day farming techniques result in wastage of water. We need to adopt water-conserving technologies, as many developed countries have done. This will also aid farming in areas with less water, and be environmentally more sustainable.

Changing mindsets: The domain of a farmer's work has to be enlarged from grain production to food processing and marketing. New technologies should be pressed into service. Over 60 per cent of India's population depends on agriculture for a living. This should be reduced to 40 per cent or less, and the people formerly employed in agriculture should ideally move to agro-processing and services, where earnings are higher. This will enable both the farmers as well as the people shifting to the new areas to become prosperous.

Diversifying products: New agricultural technologies have to be pressed into service. Farmers need to be encouraged to move to producing crops where they have a natural advantage, and for which there is good demand. Animal husbandry and growing cash crops are two of the many new areas which are emerging.

The important technologies required for the Second Green Revolution include:

1. **Soil matching:** Using modern sensors, it is now possible to examine the soil and find out its characteristic deficiencies and excesses. If there are excessive salts, these have to be neutralized with chemical or biological treatment. Some deficiencies, such as that of zinc or phosphorus, can be rectified by adding supplements, just as you might have vitamin pills! Another aspect of soil matching is that it becomes possible to say which crop would grow best on that soil, and farmers can devote themselves to growing that crop, provided of course that there is a demand in the market for it.

2. **Water technologies:** The amount of water used should be minimized. Technologies like drip irrigation, at its most sophisticated using microelectronics circuits to control irrigation, should be increased. We should heed the example of Israel, a country with practically no rain, which is today a leader in many agricultural products and milk production.

3. **Crop rotation and better seeds:** Farmers must more systematically implement age-old ways of increasing production. For example, multiple cropping, which gives greater yield from the same land, and judicious crop rotation, which helps in protecting the soil. There are now high-yielding and hybrid seeds available, which give new and varied types of genetically improved crops. Simple biotechnological tools—like tissue culture—help to improve growth of vegetables like potatoes. Farmers can also look at new crops, such as herbs, as possible areas of diversification.

4. **Fertilizers and pesticides**: When I met Norman Borlaug, who won the 1970 Nobel Peace Prize for his work in agriculture that helped to feed many of the starving people of the world, he stated that fertilizers are a must for modern agriculture. But if one properly tests the soil and controls irrigation, fertilizer usage can be reduced to a minimum. As chemical fertilizers are often expensive and polluting, we can look at using organic fertilizers. Biotechnology can help in creating these. Similarly, pesticide usage can be minimized through biological control of pests.

5. **Animal husbandry**: India is one of the top milk-producing nations of the world. However, there is difficulty in exporting milk as we do not meet certain international standards in bacterial control. Agencies like the TIFAC have worked to establish such standards, especially in Punjab, Karnataka and Andhra Pradesh. Such standards need to be adopted nationally.

6. **Phytosanitary conditions**: In order to reach export markets, it is important that all agricultural produce—whether poultry, animal or plants—meet certain international cleanliness levels in chemical, bacterial and other residues. Indian agricultural produce does not always meet these standards, as a result of which these products cannot reach export markets. If Indian villages have to prosper, the produce of the farms have to reach the high-value export markets. To achieve such phytosanitary conditions, the technologies involved are not complex, but farmers have to be made aware of these and provided with the tools necessary to achieve these.

7. **Cash crops**: Crops like tea, cotton and spices have the potential to be high earners. It is essential that these are given the technological attention they require. New cash crops also need to be explored. For example, in

Uttaranchal, farmers in collaboration with agricultural researchers, have made geranium into an important mass-produced crop that yields valuable revenue. Aloe vera, which grows in abundance in the wild in India, is much in demand internationally. It is only one of many herbs which may sell well internationally. Vanilla beans and flowers are other cash crops which yield high incomes.

There are many specialists at different agricultural universities who have been working on these areas. For example, TIFAC has been providing information and help to the farmers in areas of Bihar, UP and Uttaranchal where the crop yield was low. In Bihar alone, between 1999 and 2003, the yield in paddy went up from 2 tons per hectare (1 hectare = 2.54 acre) to 5.8 tons per hectare, and the yield in wheat went up from 2 tons a hectare to almost 5. This caused dramatic changes in the income of the farmers.

Education through scientific information

The traditional image of the Indian farmer is that he is poor and uneducated. He has no access to the new developments in farming; he may be even unaware that there are any new developments. This traditional image is no longer true. With so many means of communication available, it is no longer a hard task to disseminate information that will help the farmer to make his work productive and remunerative.

Information technology and tele-consultancy: It is important to maintain an updated and enriched database of region-specific agricultural information so that this can be shared with the farmer who needs it. Such information can range from details about soil enrichment and seed selection to information about when the monsoons will arrive. Information about the market, and the kind of prices different agricultural products are fetching in both the national and international markets, will enable farmers to decide what crops to grow. Information technology (IT) makes it easy to store and share such data.

District- and panchayat-level institutions need to take a lead in acquiring the latest information using IT as a tool and making it available to the farmers in their native language. Agricultural universities can assist in the process. Over time, a databank of information can be built up which will be very useful for all farmers. There is scope for entrepreneurial work in providing such services, which will yield good income.

Agro-processing, transportation, storage and marketing systems

In the past decade or so, Indian shops have increasingly become flooded by processed foods of various kinds. As a result, there has been a rise in demand for agricultural products which are used in the food processing industry. There are such a wide variety of processed foods that people now eat, which were not common, say, thirty years back. Do you know cornflakes that you have for breakfast need a special kind of corn? And that the potato chips or wafers that you eat need a special kind of potato? There are many manufacturers producing these and so it makes sense for farmers to grow these.

India is the largest producer of fruit in the world (annual production 46 million tons in 2002). However, more than 30 per cent of the fruit is wasted as it cannot reach the market and there is limited scope for processing it. In the US, 70 per cent of the fruit produced is processed, in Malaysia 83 per cent. In India this is a mere 2 per cent. Recently, however, with the increasing popularity of processed fruit juices in the market, this is improving.

Some agricultural produce have very short shelf-lives if they are unprocessed. Processing helps to preserve and add value to agricultural products such as rice, wheat, vegetables, fruits, potato and fish. As a result of preserving and proper refrigeration, these products can reach more people without getting spoilt. This ensures less loss for the producers as well as better food for people. Farmers' incomes will increase. That is why agro-processing is an integral part of the Second Green Revolution.

Processing is especially important for dairy farming. Milk needs to be pasteurized in order to last for any length of time. It is therefore also essential that such processing facilities are available reasonably close at hand to the dairy farms.

> I read a book called *An Unfinished Dream* by the milkman of India, Dr Verghese Kurien. He says, 'It was by chance I became a dairy man.' He heard a British expert's say that 'the sewer water of London is superior to the milk of Bombay'. This served as a challenge to young Kurien, who started the Anand cooperative in Gujarat in the 1950s. He has taken dairying from strength to strength over the decades so that today India is the world's second-largest milk producer.

However, it is not enough merely to grow good crops. In order to reach the markets where they will be sold or processed, it is important that a good transportation network is built.

Management of agricultural waste is another important area which can turn out to be a source for revenue generation. Agricultural waste should be put to use by developing appropriate and cost-effective technologies, such as generation of biogas, and production of vermi-compost and paper, as well as other products.

The way forward

The contribution of agriculture to India's GDP has reduced from 39 to 22 per cent in the period 1979–2004. In the same period, manufacturing and services have grown from 24 to 27 per cent and 37 to 51 per cent respectively. The percentage of people in agriculture has come down from 64 to 54. By 2020, our employment pattern should be 44 per cent in agriculture, 21 per cent in manufacturing and 35 per cent in the services sector.

This will happen for two reasons. Agricultural technology would assist the future farmers so that they need to hire fewer workers. Simultaneously, there will be growth in the services, agro-processing and industrial sectors, and people will move to these sectors to earn more money.

The conventional role of the Indian farmer will be changed from a producer of food to an entrepreneur engaged in processing and marketing of international-standard farm products and derivatives.

Some products have demand in the international market, such as pickles, chutneys, fruit pulp, frozen and dehydrated fruits and vegetables. In addition, India also has the potential to export more meat and poultry products—it already exports egg powder, frozen egg yolk and other egg products to Europe, Japan and other parts of the world. There are also new Indian agricultural products which have international demand, such as processed fruits and vegetables, and fish products. The value-addition through processing will bring much-needed money to India's farmers.

The Second Green Revolution has changed agriculture from something practised only by farmers in villages to something that will require the best minds in technology, management, marketing and services. For Indian youths today, who want to take up new challenges and put their technological knowledge to meaningful use, the farming sector offers many interesting choices.

Materials and the Future

If you think about the development of human civilization, you will find that the pace of social and economic growth has been closely related to the proficiency with which people have been able to use the materials and chemicals in the world around them.

In the beginning, this was through keen observation and trial and error. Thousands of years ago, men and women discovered, perhaps by accident, that they could hunt more easily if they sharpened rocks into weapons. They discovered that certain herbs helped to heal wounds. Once they discovered these properties of the materials around them, they remembered these and started using them. Their knowledge of these few things was slowly extended to others. As more and more knowledge was accumulated, human civilization as we know it today developed.

Think about all the things you take for granted, as a normal part of life. Do you know it was only about two hundred years ago that man started using coal and oil as energy sources to run machinery? The railways were invented. As a result, man could transport raw materials from far away to create new products and also sell them in distant places. It thus became very easy for goods to be transported, made easier still by the advent of the automobile and the aeroplane. Today, you can talk to people across the world from wherever you are—home, office, on a bus. But mobile phones were commercially available only from 1987. The first mobiles were available in India from 1994–95—and there were over

10 million users by 2002!

> Even something which seems as simple as a matchbox was only invented in the late nineteenth century—less than 120 years ago. Imagine how difficult it was to light a fire before that!

Some ten years ago, the Internet became widely used. A vast world of information became available on the computer at the click of a mouse. As a result, knowledge flows so much easier. Sitting at your desk in India, you can find out about events and technologies all over the world. When I was writing this book, it was so much quicker for me to check the facts. Ten years ago, it would have taken me ten times as long to write it, as I would have to go to many libraries and talk to many different people to get the same amount of information. The creation of so much technology is dependent on the creation of the advanced materials which are used to create computers, fibre optic cables, scanners and printers.

Just imagine then, how different the world can be a hundred years from now! At the present rate of growth, in twenty years we can have trains that will travel from Delhi to Mumbai in a few hours—there is talk already of trains that can move as fast as planes using electromagnetic technology, robots in every home that can do the housework, and computers that will write down your homework as you talk! In this exciting world of rapid change, you have many wonderful opportunities to change the world and change India, if you can think out of the box and work with technology!

The magic of new materials

There are so many new materials available nowadays which our grandparents did not have access to. Our houses are full of modern materials: stainless steel, fibre glass, plastics, musical and audio-visual materials. In the world outside, there are so many new materials as well: lightweight, high-performance alloys help us build aircraft, satellites, launch vehicles and missiles and various kinds of plastics. Think of all the things in your daily life which are made of plastic—and imagine a world without them. The better use a country can make of its materials and chemicals, the more prosperous it will be.

You must have heard of Agni, India's indigenously produced intermediate-range ballistic missile, first test-fired in May 1989. For Agni, we at the Defence Research and Development Organization (DRDO) developed a new, very light material called carbon-carbon.

One day, an orthopaedic surgeon from the Nizam Institute of Medical Sciences in Hyderabad visited my laboratory. He lifted the material and found it so light that he took me to his hospital and showed me his patients—little girls and boys who had polio or other problems, as a result of which their legs could not function properly. The doctors helped them to walk in the only way they could—by fitting heavy metallic callipers on their legs. Each calliper weighed over 3 kg, and so the children walked with great difficulty, dragging their feet around.

The doctor who had taken me there said to me, 'Please remove the pain of my patients.'

In three weeks, we made these Floor Reaction Orthosis 300-gram callipers and took them to the orthopaedic centre. The children could not believe their eyes! From dragging around a 3-kg load on their legs, they could now move around freely with these 300-gram callipers. They began running around! Their parents had tears in their eyes.

An ex-serviceman from a middle-class family in Karnataka wrote to us, after reading about how we had assisted polio-affected children. He inquired if something could be done for his twelve-year-old daughter who was suffering from residual polio of the leg and was forced to drag herself with a 4.5-kg calliper made out of wood, leather and metallic strips. Our scientists invited the father and daughter to our laboratory in Hyderabad, and together with the orthopaedic doctors at the Nizam's Institute of Medical Sciences, designed a Knee Ankle Foot Orthosis weighing merely 400 grams. The girl's walking almost returned to normal using this. The parents wrote to us a couple of months later that the girl had learned cycling and started going to school on her own.

These new materials can also help in making life easier in ways that were not thought of when they were being invented. The DRDO has developed at least fifteen promising life science spin-off technologies from what were originally defence projects, some of them missile programmes.

Is it necessary to have material resources in order to be a developed country?

Many developed countries possess rich material resources—the US (copper, gold, lead, lithium, molybdenum, rare earths, zinc, among others), Russia (gold, iron ore, lead and nickel), China (gold, oil, iron ore, molybdenum and rare earths) and Australia (coal, iron, oil, bauxite, copper, gold, lead and nickel) are all examples of this. However, the presence of material resources does not ensure that a country can become developed.

Many African nations have rich mineral deposits. This was one of the reasons why many European nations colonized different parts of Africa in the nineteenth century. Coal was discovered and mined mainly for export. Later, other minerals were discovered—gold, bauxite, manganese, copper, iron, tin, uranium, crude oil and gas. South Africa has half the world's gold mines and substantial portions of the earth's diamonds. Zimbabwe, Congo, Zambia, Ethiopia, Rwanda and Namibia all have substantial mineral resources. However, despite this, Africa remains poor today because the resources are not developed to create higher value products within the country. The raw ores are purchased by foreign countries who make to them into metals and then manufacture products and sell to the whole world, including to the country which provided the ore. Manufactured goods sell for more money than the ore. This process is known as value addition, and it helps the countries manufacturing the finished products to become wealthy. When you sell a mineral in its unprocessed state, or after some preliminary processing, then the prices are much lower and the number of people who are earning their living through the processing is much smaller. If one sells finished products, then prices are higher and more people can earn a living through the process.

One of the ironies of selling a material in an unprocessed state is that then theoretically the country could be buying it back in a processed state again, but at a higher price. That is, for example, if a country exports pig iron, and imports cars, the cars it is purchasing at high price could be made of the same iron that it had exported. The more advanced a state of processing the material is sold at, the more the money which accrues to the country.

Japan has almost no mineral deposits. However, Japan imports iron ore and exports it as value-added steel, builds ships and is one of the economic and technological leaders of the world. So are South Korea and Taiwan, who do not have sizeable mineral deposits.

While materials as raw ores are important and cost money to buy, they are much cheaper than the finished product which can be made with that material. You can see examples of that in your daily life. For example, compare the prices of potatoes in the vegetable market and of a packet of chips in the grocery store. A packet, which contains, say, 100 grams of potato chips, will cost, say, Rs 20. If you buy 100 grams of potatoes in the vegetable market it may cost you only Re 1. When you buy a shirt, it might cost you anything from Rs 100 to much, much more. Yet the cotton from which the thread is spun and the cloth is woven would cost you much less.

It is the same when it comes to larger-scale productions and countries. Countries which sell the raw materials—cotton, iron, tin—would earn much less than countries which sell the finished goods. To make finished goods you need technological strengths in material and manufacturing.

Thus, the crucial factor in determining a country's level of development is not possession of material resources, but what the people can do with the resources. The countries that have mastered the technologies to develop and process the resources into expensive products, which they can use themselves or others can buy from them, will earn much more than nations which merely sell the resources. This is how the economic strength of countries that master technologies is built up.

With economic strength comes political strength in global forums. As we have discussed earlier, the powerful countries nowadays are not those which have conquered territory, but those which have lots of wealth through technology and trade. With their economic strength, countries can try to dominate other countries politically.

There are many interesting stories about how countries that have technological strengths in making products out of ores deny these products to the countries which supplied the ore in the first place. During the 1970s, when we were developing SLV-3, India's first satellite launch system, we needed certain beryllium products for this project. Beryllium is one of the lightest of all metals and has one of the highest melting points of light metals. It is used in high-speed aircraft, missiles, spacecrafts and communication satellites, among other things.

A US company that was manufacturing the beryllium products we needed refused to supply them to us. A Japanese company was making some parts of these products, but they too refused. Trying to figure out a solution, I started to find out more about beryllium. I discovered that India has one of the world's richest stocks of beryllium ore. India also had the technology to convert this ore into metal, and also to shape it according to the needs of the project. We, in the Indian

Space Research Organization (ISRO), in partnership with the Department of Atomic Energy (DAE), solved the problem of beryllium. It is now manufactured in India.

This denial of beryllium products was an early lesson for me: if you don't have the technology, your natural resources are of no use to you.

India's Material Resources

India has excellent mineral resources, which are used for manufacturing a wide range of essential things.

Iron: About 98 per cent of iron ore is used to make steel, one of most useful materials ever created. While the other uses for iron ore and iron account for only a very small amount of the consumption, they are wide-ranging and include magnets, car parts, medicines, printing inks, plastics and fertilizers. Steel is essential for all kinds of construction: houses, trains, cars, machinery, vessels and even domestic utensils.

Did you know? There is an iron column near Delhi's Qutb Minar which has stood out in the open for about sixteen centuries and shows no signs of deterioration. In being able to manufacture iron of such composition, India's industry was about fifteen centuries ahead of Europe! We need to become similar world leaders in modern steel technology!

Manganese ore: Steel becomes harder when it is alloyed with manganese, therefore the most important use of the mineral is in the manufacture of steel. It is also used in the manufacture of dry cell batteries and to prepare some chemicals.

Titanium: Titanium is a strong, lightweight metal often used in aeroplanes and in several applications as a substitute for steel. It is considered the material of the twenty-first century. When titanium combines with oxygen, it forms titanium dioxide, a brilliant white pigment used in paint, paper and plastics. Titanium is also used for diverse applications such as dental fillings and artificial hip joints. We have some of the largest ores of titanium in our country (37 per cent of world resources). However, we need to work harder at developing and using this valuable resource.

Titanium is a wonder metal. It is as strong as steel but much lighter. Unlike aluminium and steel, it is corrosion resistant. It is, for example, resistant to salt water, which corrodes most materials. In many chemical plants and electric power stations in coastal areas, using titanium means that there are no power failures due to breakdowns! Human blood is also very corrosive, and steel plates in the body need to be changed. However, titanium plates are not affected by blood and do not need to be changed.

Aluminium: Bauxite is the main source of aluminium. The lightness, strength and corrosion resistance of aluminium are important considerations in its applications. It is used in packaging, transportation, construction, electrical appliances and other products. India is rich in aluminium ores.

Rare earth: The rare earths are a relatively abundant group of elements consisting of scandium, yttrium and the lanthanide series. They are used for a variety of different applications. Most rare earth compounds are used in automobile catalytic converters (which burn fuel more efficiently and reduce pollution) and as a catalyst in refining petroleum. They are also used in glass polishing and ceramics, permanent magnets and alloys in metals. Thorium can be a nuclear fuel and can redefine the future of energy in India. There are also rare earth magnets which are used, for example, in miniaturized earphones. India has several rare earth deposits.

Beryl ores: Beryllium is very light and has a high melting point. Its alloys are used mostly for aerospace products, automobiles, computers, oil and gas drilling equipment and telecommunications. It is also used in the defence industry and in nuclear reactors as a neutron absorbent. Beryllium salts are used in fluorescent lamps, in X-ray tubes and as a deoxidizer in bronze metallurgy.

Coal: An all-important source of energy, which India has in plenty.

India's mining programme does not reflect the diversity of minerals available in the country. Eighty per cent of our mining is in coal and the balance 20 per cent is in various metals and other raw materials, such as gold, copper, iron, lead, bauxite, zinc and uranium. India's mining sector has not grown as much as it could have and there is much scope for working on value additions.

But, as has been discussed before, what is more important than the availability of natural resources is how we can use technology to improve them, utilize them in national development and sell them as exports, besides meeting our domestic needs.

It is important to remember that all mineral resources are finite, and will come to an end one day. Therefore, we should always aim to produce the final product in order to ensure that the maximum income accrues for the country as a result of value addition.

Technology and value addition are of prime importance for the prosperity of the nation. Value addition is a potential employment spinner. We have to work hard in value addition techniques in our manufacturing industries, as in all sectors. Let us look at one important industry in India—the steel industry—to see how technology has affected its development in the last decades.

The Steel Industry in India

Steel, an alloy of iron and carbon, can be produced in many forms. At the lowest end of the range of iron products is pig iron, which is used in the process of steel making. Steel is also manufactured as various kinds of alloys (mixtures of two or more kinds of different metals or non-metals) which are specifically made with different uses in mind. For example, alloys of steel and tungsten are used to make cutting tools and precision instruments. Steel can be manufactured in different forms—as wires, sheets, rods and bars, again to suit the different end uses.

It is essential that India produces enough steel for its domestic demand, so that we have enough for our needs without importing. Ideally, we should also be able to export steel and steel products to other countries.

A brief history of the modern steel industry

'The nation which gains control of iron soon acquires the control of gold'—these were the words that inspired a young Jamsetji Nusserwanji Tata envisage a bold new dream for India.

J.N. Tata set up the first steel plant in India in 1907, in what was later to be known as Jamshedpur. In 1912, the first ingot of steel rolled out in India by Asia's first and India's largest integrated private sector steel company. In 1916, during World War I, the Tatas exported 2,400 km of steel rails to Mesopotamia.

Public sector: owned wholly or partly by the government

Private sector: owned and managed by non-government individuals or groups

After Independence, successive governments placed great emphasis on the development of the Indian steel industry. In 1953, the Indian government entered into an agreement with a West German firm to set up the steel plant at Rourkela. In 1960 came the steel plant at Durgapur, and in 1965, the steel plant at Bokaro in collaboration with the US. Initially, most of the plants were in the public sector, though there were small ones in the private sector.

In the last decade, the government has started seeking private sector investment in the steel industry. As a result, there are now many new steel plants. In 1991, there were six major steel plants—of which five were in the public sector—and 180 minor steel plants.

How has the world's steel production grown over the years?

Year	Quantity (in million tons)
1970	595
1980	716
1990	770
2000	848
2001	850
2002	902
2003	965

To understand how India's steel production compares with other countries, let us look at the table that follows:

Country	2003 tonnage	2002 tonnage	2001 tonnage
China	220.1	181.6	150.9
Japan	110.5	107.7	102.9
US	90.4	92.3	90.1
Russia	62.7	59.8	59.0
South Korea	46.3	45.4	43.9
Germany	44.8	45.0	44.8
Ukraine	36.9	33.4	33.1
India	33.6	30.6	29.2
Brazil	31.1	29.6	26.7
Italy	26.1	26.1	26.6

All figures in million tons

While India has started exporting, it still remains quite low in the list of international exporters. However, numbers are growing. Also, in terms of exports, we are exporting more of semi-finished steel, stainless steel and pig iron rather than ore.

Year	Total production	Export
2001–2	30.6	2.7
2002–3	33.6	3.7

All figures in million tons

The fact that such an improvement has come at a time of intense global competition is commendable. But our potential is much more. Look at the performance of an Indian—Lakshmi Narayan Mittal. He is the owner of largest steel-manufacturing empire in the world. Many of the steel plants are managed by Indian professionals. We need to create an environment for Indian entrepreneurs to think and act boldly.

Other materials and technologies

While steel is a basic material for modern manufacturing and industrialization, India also needs to have mastery over new alloys of steels, aluminium and titanium. We also need to master newer techniques, like surface engineering, where a surface modification gives a material new properties. For example, when we coat a simple aluminium alloy with iridium, it makes the material wear-resistant, which ordinary aluminium is not. You can see this in your watch—when it has a coating or glass which is scratch-resistant.

Various forms of plastics, ceramics and composite materials are crucial for the modern world, to make habitats or machines. Ceramics, which we normally associate with washbasins or teacups, in an advanced form is used for energy-efficient engines.

> Ceramics are very strong structural materials. They can be made in different structural forms called ceramic-matrix composites. These have great strength but are light because of the hollow space within. In structure (atomic), they resemble a beehive!

Internationally, manufacturing technologies are growing more complex by the day. Today, nanotechnology, the technology of building objects by the placement of individual atoms or molecules, or where at least one dimension is measured by nanometres (one billionth of a metre) is a part of manufacturing. Indian industries have to master new technologies, including nanotechnology, to succeed in modern-day manufacturing.

> Nanotechnology is a future technology that will have a large number of applications in materials and manufacturing, medicine and healthcare, environment and energy, biotechnology and agriculture, space and defence. The essence of nanotechnology is the ability to work at the molecular level to create fundamentally new molecular structures.

The way forward

Materials and manufacturing are the core of modern human civilization. Over the years, like civilization itself, manufacturing has evolved, absorbed new technologies and created new cutting-edge products. More and more products are being manufactured today—as human civilization becomes more dependent on technology.

Chemical Industries and Biotechnology

The use of chemicals and chemical products affect our lives in several ways, direct and indirect. Fertilizers, organic or inorganic nitrogenous substances which boost growth of plants, and pesticides, to control fungus and insects, are needed for agriculture. Petrol, diesel and plastics are essential parts of modern-day living. There are many other household items we take for granted for food, sanitation and hygiene: salt, textiles, detergents, cosmetics, beverages, medicines, packed foods, paints, leather goods, books and newspapers. These are all essential chemical products which we need to live life the way we are used to.

At the same time, the manufacture and use of these chemicals may create other challenges. Chemicals can have negative effects, if wrongly used. They can cause air pollution, soil degradation, they can pollute rivers and lakes, and threaten marine life by pollution and by creating imbalances in the environment. So should chemicals be regarded as modern demons? As in every other field of human activity, science and technology can also be used for wrongful purposes. Sometimes, accidents can occur. But it is important to remember that, barring the occasional lack of ethics on the part of a scientist or a business group, if the ill effects are known at the time of development of a process or product, that activity is always abandoned. Modern science and technological methods and business practices have built-in ethical codes. Chemicals or medicines are deployed only after rigorous tests, field trials and due certification processes. Modern biotechnology can make chemical products which were earlier not environmentally friendly 'cleaner' by replacing certain chemical processes.

> A **chemical** may be defined as a substance that is produced or used in a process involving changes to atoms and molecules. The term is more broadly used to mean a substance.

Certain chemicals have herbal substitutes. Some chemical pesticides, for example, can be replaced by organic, herbal ones—such as neem or tobacco. Many chemicals are extracted from herbs. Thus the chemical industry and India's herbal wealth are intricately related.

Strategies for Chemical Industries

India has ample resources for developing chemical-based industries. There are certain chemical industries in which India has traditionally been strong in, and we also have well-trained scientists and technologists. It is essential that India learns to make full use of its resources through constant technological adaptations. The modern challenge is to create a 'clean' chemical industry where processes do not cause pollution.

India is rich in herbs, germ plasmas and micro-organisms. This biodiversity means that there are ample resources for developing one particular facet of the chemical industry based on natural products.

> **Biodiversity** is the variety of all life forms: the different plants, animals and micro-organisms, their genes and the ecosystems of which they are a part.

India has an amazing biodiversity due to the vast land

area, with its many geographic and climate zones. There is mountain and desert, vast plains and oceans, rivers, lakes and ponds, and many different kinds of forests—deciduous, temperate and tropical—and plant life. India is endowed with a vast coastline with marine resources and oil wealth.

However, what is happening is that industrially developed countries are importing these bio-resources in raw form and adding value to them for export to developing countries, including India, as special seeds, medicines and bio-materials. Moreover, they secure patents on these products which give special rights. The scenario is similar to that with raw mineral ores and value-added finished products that we discussed in the previous chapter. To convert herbs and plants to modern medicines or cosmetics requires scientific and technological knowledge and special manufacturing techniques. Instead of merely exporting of such resources and importing final products at high cost, India should utilize local technology to transform its natural resources into value-added products for domestic requirements and also for export.

We also need to learn how to maximize the earnings from every process. In processing chemicals, there are often by-products created. We must learn to utilize these by-products as far as possible, instead of creating wastes that add to pollution. This transformation of potentially harmful waste into an useful produce leads to what is known as a clean chemical process.

In the early years of the sugar industry, for example, the focus was on maximizing sugar output. The waste products, except for molasses—the thick, dark syrup which drains from sugar in the process of manufacture and is used as a sweetener for various products—were not used. Even bagasse, the crushed outer stalks of sugar cane, was burnt. Nowadays, bagasse is used for making paper and for co-generation of electricity. There are about a dozen chemicals which can be made from other waste products, such as oxalic acid (which is a rust remover and wood bleaching agent). Action is under way to recover these as well.

Earlier, India used to import polyester yarn for making fabrics. This yarn is made from Purified Terephthalic Acid (PTA), a by-product of petrochemical purification. Now, as more oil refineries are set up in India, polyester yarn can be manufactured locally. Other by-products of oil refineries include plastic, nylon, washing powders and farming chemicals.

The bulk of the chemicals in India are still produced in the small-scale sector. So far the chemical industry has been focussed on imported process technology. However, strong research and development (R&D), engineering and equipment manufacturing have led to adaptation of imported technology for local use, as well as the development of indigenous technology. The target is to achieve our own process technologies for most of the products by 2020.

Our biological wealth and the chemical industry

We depend on India's amazing biodiversity for our survival and quality of life. The most significant impediment to the conservation, management and economic utilization of this biodiversity is our lack of knowledge about how to use the resources in modern systems.

It so happens that such biodiversity largely occurs in developing countries which are not yet technologically advanced. We are lucky in that we have both the bio-resources as well as technological and industrial strength. But this strength has to be further increased and focussed on sustained economical use of the resources. This will help not only the chemical industry but also the agricultural sector which could cultivate the herbs and other plants needed.

India has great reserves of traditional knowledge, from ancient classical texts as well as from tribal sources. It is only recently that we are coming to realize fully the wealth of knowledge contained in these texts and practices. Many ancient knowledge bases, such as in tribal societies, are only now being researched. Large amounts of data on traditional systems of medicine, the use of herbs, and even metallurgy have been gathered. This traditional knowledge can be newly used with modern technological tools with suitable modification to suit the modern context.

The process of documentation and recording has to be carefully carried out so that no material is lost. This will help us to chart out and understand our biodiversity, protect it, and forge new technologies out of it.

Worldwide, there is a movement towards what are called 'new age' cures—which for us are simple age-old traditional treatments. Yoga and ayurveda are now getting popular across the globe. This gives a great opportunity for the Indian herbal industry to develop and sell its products internationally. But we need to use modern scientific techniques in organizing and marketing them.

> Some ayurvedic medicines made in India are now being sold all over the world. These include various tonics with ingredients such as hinsra (medicinal capers), kasani (chicory), arjuna and kakamachi (black nightshade) which are believed to have beneficial effects.

India is blessed with more than sixteen bioclimates which enable us to produce a variety of herbal plants. A combination of traditional knowledge, modern biotechnology and the natural diversity could create excellent products which would sell internationally. There are also many highly trained practitioners of the traditional systems whose knowledge and expertise could be used to develop a clean industry which could become one of the primary engines of growth and prosperity for the country.

Energy-related chemical industries

From an economic point of view, perhaps the most essential chemicals are those used to generate energy, most importantly petroleum and natural gas. The by-products of fuel generation give us other important chemicals which are used as lubricants for cars and engines, plastics and fertilizers.

India has made rapid strides in this vital sector. The Oil and Natural Gas Commission, Indian Oil Corporation and Reliance Industries are three of the companies which have done much for developing this part of the chemical industry.

India has limited resources of gas. As we have technical expertise in this field, we have also started doing oil exploration abroad, working with countries like Sri Lanka, Iran, Sudan and Norway.

There is also exploration into alternative fuels—such as coal in a gasified state, biomass and biodiesel. These are discussed in the ninth chapter.

The pharmaceutical industry

The pharmaceutical sector is very crucial in any country, as the healthcare available in the country is dependent on it. Before Independence, India lacked pharmaceutical plants. Even simple medicines that were not part of any of the indigenous medical systems were imported.

India could not have sustained a modern healthcare system—which has saved millions of deaths through vaccination, antibiotics and other drugs—through imports alone. Development of this sector to ensure that medicines were freely available at affordable prices to people was made a priority. As a result, today this sector has shown truly outstanding growth, so much so that Indian companies are now exporting drugs to the rest of the world.

One of the problems of the Indian pharmaceutical industry is that few, if any, drugs are invented here. They are mainly produced under licence. In present-day global economy, whoever patents a medicine gets global rights (known as intellectual property rights) over it.

Indian companies are now emerging with new products. You can read more about these from economic and financial newspapers and websites. This is an area in which those who have scientific and technological aptitude can make a real difference to the lives of people.

Biotechnology

Biotechnology has recently risen to prominence, though research has been underway for the past five decades. Biotechnology opens new ways of understanding and shaping nature and human life. Some of the areas in which biotechnology has a role to play are agriculture, agro-processing, bio waste disposal, forestry, animal husbandry, poultry farming and pharmaceuticals.

The development of biotechnology has given a fillip to many herbal and plant-based products. It is now possible to genetically alter the natural properties of plants and seeds to maximize their utility.

Biotechnology has revolutionized the chemical industry. For example, earlier, removing the hair from animal skins (known as tanning) was a laborious process involving the use of lime and strong salts which was injurious to the health of workers and caused environmental pollution. Modern biotechnology has transformed the process into a simple and pollution-free operation, where workers are no longer suffering. The Central Leather Research Institute has been working to pass on this technology to small tanneries.

One of the problems associated with mining was that traditional mining, smelting and refining procedures generated toxic wastes and caused environmental pollution. Biotechnology has come up with a new method, known as bio-leaching, which involves the extraction of metals from ores or concentrates using components found readily within the environment, such as water, air and micro-organisms that 'eat away' at the ore. These processes cause much less environmental pollution.

All these biotechnological and genetic engineering processes have to be done with great care and caution. A microbe whose behaviour is not completely known to us can create undesirable side effects. Therefore, many tests have to be conducted by scientists and technologists before these processes can be used on a large scale.

Biotechnology and IT in tandem have created new areas of research and development. One such area is genomics, the study of all of the particles that make up DNA. Among the many uses of genomics is that it helps in the study of the relationship between genes and diseases, whether they are caused by defect or deficiency, and therefore we acquire a greater sense of how to treat diseases.

The role of biotechnology in healthcare is significant. It has resulted, for example, in the creation of new vaccines, such as one for hepatitis B, which is often hard to cure.

It has also made possible precision treatment of diseases. In most illnesses, only one part of your body is affected. However, oral medication means that the whole body absorbs the medicine. Biotechnology, in combination with nanotechnology, makes it possible to medicate only the diseased cells with controlled releases of drugs. This is called targetted therapy.

Biotechnology has thus been transforming the way in which the chemical industry works. The chemical industry is now becoming cleaner, with less adverse environmental effect.

In addition, biotechnology provides new opportunities for India's strong traditional knowledge systems, and helps to create a competitive advantage for India in these fields.

The way forward

As you can see, the diverse areas of growth in the chemical industry offer much scope for new endeavour. Biotechnology is transforming the way things work, and providing new opportunities, in addition to the existing ones, for India's chemical industry to become a global giant.

Manufacturing for the Future

When you hear the term 'manufacturing', it often conjures up images of smoky steel mills, clanking machinery and huge furnaces belching out smoke and fire. However, today manufacturing can mean something very different, as we have discussed earlier.

India has a rich tradition in manufacturing. Traditional Indian skills in medicine, metallurgy, construction, textiles, hydraulics and shipbuilding were an integral part of our innovativeness in ancient and medieval times. But when it came to a transition from an artisans to large-scale production with energy-driven machines like steam mills or diesel engines, India lagged behind. The effects of the Industrial Revolution in the western world in the eighteenth and nineteenth centuries, which made technology, rather than individual skill, the key to successful manufacturing, took a very long time to reach India.

The key to success in the modern world lies in superior technology. Technology can be defined as the application of scientific knowledge for practical purposes, especially in industry. Any country which has superior technology—which improves speed, reduces costs, or makes the product better in some way—will be successful in selling that product worldwide, as it will be able to achieve better quality at a lower price. The invention of the horse collar in the Middle Ages led to major changes in agricultural methods, and was as much of a technological advance as the invention of

Bessemer furnaces (in 1856), which made it possible to manufacture steel of a better quality and at a lower price than ever before.

The term technology encompasses techniques as well as the machines that may or may not be necessary to apply them. It includes ways to make chemical reactions occur, ways to breed fish, eradicate weeds, and almost any other process or method of doing something that you can think of. Changes in technology bring about dramatic changes in the way people live and work and think. Think of computers—how different our lives were without them!

Indian manufacturing has been revitalized in the recent past. You can see this in the range of cars, mainly manufactured in India, which you see on the streets of most cities nowadays. There are some areas where India has a lot of potential but where the pace of manufacturing needs to pick up, such as machine tools and electronic hardware.

India has the potential to become a global manufacturing centre, the world's workshop, as it were. We have people skilled in engineering and technology. Modern machines have a large degree of automation, where the process is supervised by computers. India can make a unique contribution to such systems through innovative software. Today, much of the process of manufacturing is driven by computers. Many machines have built-in computers that guide their performance. In this chapter, we will focus on the impact of computers and software on manufacturing.

The most advanced technological processes are nowadays carried out far from assembly lines or open hearths of the factories we know from old films. In electronics, space technology and most of the new industries, relative silence and clean surroundings are characteristic, even essential. The assembly line, with armies of men to carry out simple routine functions, is more or less a thing of the past. In many cases, such simple routine functions are now carried out by machines.

Earlier, when a new product was being designed, much time and effort would be dedicated to creating dummies or prototypes, in the factory or the laboratory. It is now often not necessary to make such prototypes to study a new product. Many new products can be designed on computers. Since we now know the way most materials behave under certain circumstances (such as reaction to heat, stress and pressure) through many years of technological experience, we can even test in a computer simulation how they will react to things. By choosing an optimum design through such simulations, computer programmes can lead on directly to the manufacturing process. Thus production is speeded up. These processes are generally called Computer-aided Design (CAD) and Computer-aided Manufacturing (CAM).

CAD/CAM engineers use CAD to create three-dimensional (involving length, breadth and depth—therefore lifelike) drawings, such as those for automobile and aeroplane parts, floor plans and maps. While it may be faster for an engineer to create an initial drawing by hand, it is much more efficient to change and distribute drawings by computer.

Rather than having to build prototypes and change components to determine the effects of tolerance ranges, engineers can use computers to simulate tests on various design features. For example, an automobile manufacturer might use CAD to calculate the wind drag or resistance on several new car-body designs without having to build physical models of each one. Today, a single computer can control banks of milling machines, lathes, welding machines and other tools, moving the product from machine to machine as each step in the manufacturing process is completed. Such systems allow easy, fast reprogramming from the computer, permitting quick implementation of design changes.

In the design stage, drafting and computer graphics techniques are combined to produce models of objects. Designers manipulate and test these models on video display screens until they incorporate the best balance of features, including ease of production and cost. The CAD information is then combined with CAM procedures through shared databases. Today, it is possible to perform the six-step 'art-to-part' process with a computer:

Step 1: Use of sketching software to capture the initial design ideas.

Step 2: Produce accurate engineering drawings.

Step 3: Rendering an accurate image of what the part will look like.

Step 4: Engineers use analysis software to ensure that the part is strong enough. This step requires lots of technological know-how.

Step 5: Production of a prototype or model.

Step 6: The CAM software controls the machine that produces the part. This will keep on changing depending on the product. The engineering team can load the right software for the product at hand.

This process has led to the concept of flexible manufacturing.

The tools used for manufacturing have also multiplied greatly, and many existing tools have now become so precise and versatile that they can be used for many different purposes. The laser (an acronym for light amplification by stimulated emission of radiation), invented in the 1960s, creates and amplifies a narrow, intense beam of light. This can be used for things as diverse as cutting heavy steel and concrete plates and delicate eye surgery. Lasers are an integral part of such familiar devices as bar-code scanners used in supermarkets, scanners, laser printers and CD players.

Technology also enables us to use the simplest things in diverse ways. When you turn on the tap at home, you get a jet of water. A similar jet of water, at ultra high pressure, can be used to cut steel, concrete or other materials. It also has other advantages in cutting over conventional saws or other cutting instruments: there is no heat, no noise, no dust and minimal shavings. New materials can also be used as tools, thanks to the new properties they acquire through modern technology. Ceramics, discussed in the previous chapter, can now also be used as tools.

Thus, manufacturing today is all about applying intelligent methods to existing processes so that work can be done as simply and swiftly as possible. India stands to gain greatly by the coupling of computers with the manufacturing process.

India has a large number of small and tiny manufacturing units, both in the organized and the so-called informal sector. They range from artisans to those with old-fashioned tools and machinery. A number of them also have basic skills and great ability to improvise with what they have.

It is important that the small-scale industries prepare themselves for competition in an era when larger units with more advanced machinery and systems could drive them out of business. This would mean working systematically to upgrade skills and machinery. They may have to exchange old machinery for new ones with enhanced capabilities, or change part of the machinery to incorporate better tools and automation.

Modern technology means that even small-scale manufacturing units can work with buyers abroad and custom-make their products for the international market. One industry where this happens widely is the fashion and home furnishings industry. Designers based in the US or in Europe design products for well-known stores. These orders are then dispatched via email or fax to small operators in different parts of India, with specifications as to materials and so on. The manufacturing is done in India, often with minimal technology, and the product is shipped to the foreign buyer.

India does not produce all these computer-controlled

machines yet, but does import them. In addition, we have the capacity to generate customized software for machines used all over the world. Our expertise in software and manufacturing can combine to create a new technological business opportunity for Indians.

Software and the Indian Success Story

The IT industry has been playing a major part in India in the last few years. The successes of the software business in Bangalore, Hyderabad and Chennai are indicative of what India as a whole can achieve by moving to new methods of manufacturing and utilizing the latest technology.

India must not only to derive benefits from the present software boom and demand, but also to prepare itself for the higher end of the market. India should dream of becoming a software leader in a decade.

When we talk about the software industry, what exactly do we mean? Well, software can comprise many different things:

Packaged applications, which everyone can use on their own computers, such as games or a drawing programme.
Operating systems for both stand-alone computers, such as the one you have at home, and networked systems, as in an office.
Software as a service, which means management tools for large networks of computers.
Enterprise software that enables efficient management of large corporations' production, sales and information systems.
Software applications and operating systems for mainframe and individual computers.
Customized software for specific industry management.

'Packaged' software is written for mass distribution, not

for the specific needs of a particular user, and may be distributed in any format—electronic download, in a disk or CD, or through a web-based service. Broad categories of packaged applications include operating systems, such as MS Office, utilities, applications and programming languages.

India's software exports have grown dramatically over the years. Indian software companies have been exporting to the US, Canada, UK, Europe, Japan, West Asia, south-east Asia, South Africa, Malaysia, Singapore, Hong Kong and Latin America. At present, almost 68 per cent of total exports are to North America.

Export of Indian ITES

Year	Exports (in US $ billion)
1999–00	4.0
2000–01	6.2
2001–02	7.6
2002–03	9.9
2003–04	13.3
2004–05	17.9 (estimated)

The new opportunities

India should start making a concerted effort to capture a share of the market in the newly emerging processes of reliable software for manufacturing, healthcare and other applications. It can also play a major role in providing services using innovative software, such as back office operations or caller IT-enabled services (ITES).

There are many success stories of the Indian software industry in terms of exports:

- CAD/CAM packages developed by the Aeronautical Development Agency (ADA) and required for the Light

Combat Aircraft (LCA) project have found application in major civilian markets and are now being marketed worldwide by a US company.

- There are many instances where Indian software has found applications in Europe and in the US, from tasks ranging from airport applications to manufacturing.
- Some software from the academic sector is being tapped by a few global giants, eventually to be integrated by them in value-added packages.

The worldwide packaged software industry for all platforms was estimated at $183 billion in 2001. India's share is still a small percentage of this. With concerted efforts by industrial houses, entrepreneurs and experts, it is believed that by 2020 India could capture about 10 to 15 per cent of the total world market for software, and emerge as an important supplier of software to companies of the developed world.

The nature of business in manufacturing sector is such that a few companies dominate the world scene due to the superiority of their technological base and organizational strengths. However, the demands of modern technology and customer preferences mean that even these global giants cannot do everything on their own. They need several sources for software, design practices, application development and so on. India's manufacturing sector can align with some of these giants to provide some of their value-added software and designs.

Some of the biggest players in the Indian software industry are:

- Tata Consultancy Services, said to be Asia's largest independent global software and services company.
- Infosys Technologies Limited, which provides consulting and IT services to clients globally.

- Wipro Technologies, an integrated corporation that offers a diverse range of products, solutions and services in systems, software, consumer care, healthcare, lighting and infrastructure technology.
- Satyam Computer Services, a diverse end-to-end IT solutions provider.

There are many vibrant small software houses as well.

These companies are also big exporters of software and software solutions. For example, in 2001–02, Tata Consultancy Services' revenue was Rs 41,870 million, and their export was Rs 38,820 million.

The way forward

Manufacturing generates a large pool of employment for people with different levels of education and skills. This is crucial for India to achieve better employment opportunities for the youth. These are challenging and exciting fields to work in today as there are so many new technologies to be mastered and innovations that you can make, both as a part of a large organization as well as a self-employed entrepreneur.

Strategic Industries

For a strong nation, which has independence and recognition in international arenas, there is need for economic strength. However, it is also crucially important to have critical technologies in crucial sectors.

When we talk about critical technologies in the Indian context, it does not mean defence weapons alone. It also means space research and atomic energy.

Why strategic industries?

It is essential for India to develop its own strategic industries.

Many people have argued that there was no need to develop a nuclear or space programme. When the programme was launched in the 1960s, the country was desperately poor and dependent on food grain imports. Many argued that the programmes had to be supported by money which could be better used for other things. But Jawaharlal Nehru and many of the founding fathers of the nation believed that a strong indigenous base in science and technology was essential for India to pull itself out of the state of underdevelopment and provide self-sustaining growth.

As Vikram Sarabhai, one of the pioneers of the space programme, said in a speech in 1968, 'There are some who question the relevance of space activities in a developing nation. To us, there is no ambiguity of purpose ... we are convinced that if we are to play a meaningful role nationally, and in the community of nations, we must be second to none in the application of advanced technologies to the problems of man and society.'

In terms of defence, space or atomic energy programmes, there are a number of items which are not that critical in the sense that they would be available relatively easily from several sources. Many of the items would not involve numerous complex operations or be very costly. Other items could be stockpiled for future consumption. We should be very selective therefore about what we term as critical technologies.

At present, only 30 per cent of India's requirements of defence supplies is produced indigenously. We must strive to raise this to at least 70 per cent by 2010. We need to achieve self-reliance in a relatively short time in defence research and development. There is no reason why we should not be able to do so.

The end of the Cold War, the state of political tension and military rivalry that existed between the US and the former USSR from the end of World War II to 1989–91, led to the markets for aerospace and defence industries in the developed world shrinking. The countries who had traditionally been strong in these industries—the US, Russia, France—are in stiff competition with one another, and do not want new countries or companies to emerge as this would reduce their share of the already small market. In this context, if we are to look at selling our satellites internationally, we need to develop the components locally so that lack of supplies cannot hinder the manufacturing plans.

India's Space Programme

India's space programme began with the launch of a sounding rocket from Thumba Equatorial Launching Station in 1963 under the supervision of Indian Committee for Space Research (INCOSPAR). The decision to build a satellite launch vehicle (SLV) was taken in 1968 and the first successful one was finally achieved in 1980. This was a solid propulsion rocket, the SLV-3, which put the Rohini satellite into orbit.

Rockets work on the principle of Newton's Third Law of Motion—every action has an equal and opposite reaction. There are two main categories of rocket engines: **liquid** and **solid**. In a liquid rocket, the **propellants** (the fuel and the oxidizer) are stored separately as liquids and are pumped into the combustion chamber of the nozzle where burning occurs. In a solid rocket, the propellants are mixed together and packed into a solid cylinder. Under normal temperature conditions, the propellants do not burn; but they will burn when exposed to heat provided by an igniter.

After the launch of the SLV, it was decided that the next step would be the Augmented Satellite Launch Vehicle (ASLV) and Polar Satellite Launch Vehicle (PSLV). The first ASLV was successfully launched in May 1992, and the first PSLV in September 1994. Later, ISRO took up Geosynchronous Satellite Launch Vehicle (GSLV), which has also become operational. During September 2004, GSLV launched an Indian-made educational satellite called Edusat.

The purpose of the launch vehicles was to put into orbit a number of satellites: the IRS for remote-sensing applications and the multipurpose INSAT (Indian National Satellite) for communications, TV broadcasts and meteorology. However, Indian satellites had been put into space by foreign launch vehicles from their respective countries before India had the capacity to launch them. The first Indian satellite was Aryabhatta, which was launched from USSR in 1975, followed by Bhaskara I and Bhaskara II in 1979 and 1981 respectively. The first IRS was launched in 1988 from USSR. The first indigenous INSAT was launched in 1992, again by a foreign launch vehicle. Other INSATs were launched from the US and French Guyana.

These days, successful flights of the indigenous PSLV and

GSLV from India have become routine. The PSLV and GSLV are the full realization of Sarabhai's dream of India making its own satellites and launching them too. This was in 1994, when an Indian launch vehicle PSLV carried an Indian satellite IRS P2 into orbit. With the IRS–PSLV combination, ISRO can think of launching remote-sensing satellites at regular intervals. The IRS is already the biggest constellation of remote-sensing satellites in the world and is set to grow even bigger. Similarly, GSLV has had recent regular successes and GSLV–INSAT series have also become fully indigenous.

The services in communication, broadcasting and meteorology are now being provided by satellites designed and built in India. Communications and direct TV broadcasting by satellite is particularly advantageous for India. The Edusat is useful for tele-education reaching all parts of the country.

Many of the elements required for launch vehicles, including materials, propellants, guidance and control machinery have been indigenously developed and are manufactured in the country. India has faced problems in the past when it tried to import cryogenic technology (which deals with the effects of extreme low temperatures) and was foiled. In a few years, India should be capable of manufacturing these launch vehicle engines to fulfil its needs.

In assembling satellites, many of the electronic components and some materials are sourced from outside the country, though India has been successful in assembling many of them.

India's satellites, launch vehicles, remote-sensing data, and other equipment for communications and meteorology have become regular operational and commercial services. They generate wealth for the country. In addition, India is going to embark upon planetary missions, beginning with a mission to the moon.

India's Nuclear Programmes

The commercial aspects of exploiting nuclear capabilities, especially for power generation, have been given high priority. Given the power situation in India and the availability of raw material for energy fuels, the use of nuclear power in some measure is inescapable though thermal and hydroelectric power are still dominant. India imports a large amount of its crude oil requirements, and pays vast amounts of foreign exchange for it. Therefore, India needs to be able to generate nuclear power on a commercial basis. Many developed countries like the US, Germany, France, Japan and Russia obtain a fairly large percentage of their electricity from nuclear energy.

There are a number of items in the atomic energy programme which are being made in India. The nation embarked on a nuclear power programme in 1958 and a nuclear explosives programme in 1968. Following a test of a nuclear device in May 1974, and five additional nuclear weapon-related tests in May 1998, India formally declared itself a nuclear-weapon state.

India's nuclear programme was conceived in the pre-Independence era by a small group of influential scientists who grasped the significance of nuclear energy and persuaded the new government after Independence to invest resources in the nuclear sector. An ambitious dual-use, three-stage nuclear programme was launched to exploit India's abundant thorium reserves. The primary focus of the programme was the production of inexpensive electricity. The complete nuclear fuel cycle—from ore mining, processing and fuel fabrication facilities, research and power reactors, spent-fuel reprocessing plants, heavy water production plants, and waste treatment and disposal facilities—was developed and this also led to India's acquiring the technical capability to build nuclear weapons.

The 1962 Indo-Chinese conflict and the subsequent Chinese nuclear test in 1964 triggered a debate within and outside the Indian government on whether India should follow suit. Ultimately, in November 1964, Prime Minister Lal Bahadur Shastri authorized theoretical work on the Subterranean Nuclear Explosion for Peaceful Purposes (SNEPP). The SNEPP project culminated in a test on 18 May 1974, which India described as a peaceful nuclear explosion (PNE).

The weapons programme was resumed in the 1980s. By May 1994, India acquired the capability to deliver nuclear weapons using combat aircraft; by 1996, Indian scientists also succeeded in developing a nuclear warhead that could be used with the army's Prithvi I ballistic missile. There were two further rounds of tests in May 1998, after which India's nuclear status was formally declared. The government declared that India would build a 'credible minimum deterrent', put a moratorium (or period of suspension) on further tests and articulated a policy of 'no-first-use', which meant that the weapons could only be used as defence in case of an attack. India has been extremely self-restrained on nuclear weapons but because a number of powerful countries possess stockpiles that they will not give up, it has become necessary for India to have such capability. Minimum essential defence will always be necessary to keep our hard-won freedom intact.

Defence Systems

India used to buy almost all its defence equipment from other countries. In 1947, there were only a few ordnance factories in the country, and developing indigenous defence equipment was not an area where there was initially a lot of investment.

However, importing defence equipment is a sensitive area.

Developed countries have been interested in making India a customer for their obsolete arms and defence equipment. They could give India and other developing countries such equipment as part of a credit package, and thus the country which needed such equipment would be perennially indebted to the 'donor'.

India has gradually developed its own manufacturing capabilities where defence equipment is concerned. At present, India has thirty-nine ordnance factories and eight public sector units, which produce a range of defence equipment including helicopters, state-of-the-art electronics, heavy trucks and tank transportation trailers, submarines, missile boats, destroyers, frigates, corvettes, fast-attack craft and guided missiles.

From the 1980s, national science and technology institutes such as ISRO, DAE and DRDO teamed up with industries to work on defence equipment. Such interaction between an R&D organization and industry increases the enthusiasm and confidence of industrial establishments and enables them to take risks and go through the rigorous quality assurance and other processes required for military systems. The DRDO launched a number of major programmes: the Integrated Guided Missile Development Project (IGMDP) (1983); the LCA (1983); the Advanced Light Helicopter (ALH); the Arjun Tank (first conceived in 1974); and a number of smaller projects, such as the Pinaka, a multiple barrel rocket launcher (MBRL). Some of these programmes have been more successful than others. BrahMos is another advanced missile system developed as a joint venture between India and Russia. It has undergone many successful trials in India and is getting ready for manufacture on a large scale.

The IGMDP: In July 1983, the government approved a programme for the development of four indigenous guided missile systems, named Prithvi short- and medium/long-range ballistic missiles, Trishul and Akash, surface-to-air missiles, Nag, the anti-tank missile, and the re-entry technology through Agni.

Prithvi is an all-weather, mobile, surface-to-surface guided missile, which can engage targets quickly and accurately over a range of 40–250 km, far beyond the range of field guns. There is a minimum reaction time, and it has the capability of being deployed at short notice at desired locations.

Three versions of Prithvi (150 km, 250 km and 350 km ranges) have been tested, and Prithvi I and Prithvi II have been inducted into the army and air force respectively. A sea version has also been tested. Agni was first tested in 1994, and in a 1998 missile test it flew close to 2,500 km.

Apart from strengthening the country to face external threats, Prithvi and Agni demonstrated that India can develop world-class high technology systems and devices by using its own strengths.

The LCA: The LCA has been in development for a long time. The programme started in 1983, and the first test flight was in January 2001. Further test flights have also been successful.

LCA is the world's smallest, lightweight, multi-role supersonic combat aircraft. It has been designed to meet the requirements of Indian Air Force as its frontline multi-mission single-seat tactical aircraft. It has a below 10 tons take-off weight (a large commercial plane has a take-off weight of about 400 tons). This aircraft provides top-class manoeuvrability and high performance.

The way forward

India needs to develop many other critical strategic systems for land, air and water (army, air force and navy). If we aim to produce 70 per cent of the defence systems in India, we can create a major manufacturing strength in our country.

Such a capability is required to provide special strengths to our armed forces. Indigenous capabilities in critical strategic system allow the armed forces to incorporate special features unique to them and which may not be available with others, thus creating a special competitive lead.

Such strengths in strategic technologies like defence, space and atomic energy have spin-off benefits in day-to-day items as well, be it a better frying pan, automobile or communication. If industries and research institutions work together with clear goals in mind, Indian industries can reap rich commercial benefits as well as improve the quality of daily life. I have told you the story of how we were able to help polio-affected children with a new material we had created for Agni.

As time goes by, the fruits of the research in strategic industries find new applications in daily life. It is a fact of life that research budgets are much higher for strategic industries, so scientists and researchers can bend their minds to developing new substances and create new electronics and software systems which can enrich our lives in ways other than those envisaged initially.

The Services Sector and the Indian Education System

The services sector includes all those economic activities other than those directly related to agriculture and manufacture (including mining). Most of the people you come across in your daily life—the shopkeeper from whom you buy food or books, the journalists who write articles in your morning newspaper, the driver of the bus who takes you to school, the teachers in school, lawyers, government officials, actors, the people who sell you tickets in the movie hall—belong to the services sector. The prevalence of a predominant services sector is a mark of a developed country.

Some examples of the services sector:

Trading	Human resources	Cultural and leisure
Marketing	development	services
Repairing	Technical and	Government service
Teaching	management consultancy	Police
Postal service	Old age care services	Tourism
Banking	Testing and calibration	Advertising
Trade promotion	services	Media

Some people argue that it is possible for a country to sustain itself through services sector alone. This may be true for small countries, but it cannot be true for a country like India, though services can and should be a major component in the economy. By engaging a large number of people in diverse activities, the services sector helps to distribute the wealth created and also create new wealth.

People used to believe that with increasing mechanization, those employed in the services sector were under threat as computers would result in they losing their jobs. But this is not true. Computers make work more efficient. For example, the computerization of railway ticketing means that the work is done more quickly, messages are sent faster from one station to the other, and you can check the status of your reservation from the comfort of your home instead of having to queue for hours at a station. There is, of course, a specific displacement of workers: a certain type of clerical staff, for example, may not be needed because computerization has helped to streamline the process. But there will still be need for people. The existing workforce must be equipped with new skills and training. The changes have to be anticipated and our workforce prepared accordingly.

As the services sector expands in scope, many new activities come up, which in turn place a new demand on the other sectors. As people earn more, the demand for better communications has resulted in the mass production of mobile phones, which creates a new sector for manufacturing. The expansion of medical care has similarly caused growth in the manufacturing sector for biomedical equipment. Thus, growth of the services sector can create growth in the economy as a whole.

The services sector allows individuals or small groups to provide specific, specialized services. For example, in the travel industry, an individual or a group can work on ticket bookings, others on hotel bookings, others on local transportation and still others as tourist guides. If they create linkages between their specific services, then consumers benefit, and each of them individually get more clients through the network. The possibilities are endless, and a person with a creative mind can always create a niche for himself or herself. There are also some parts of the services sector which still has gaps to be filled, such as insurance in its more specialized forms, as for agricultural crops and rural health.

Perhaps the most crucial area in the services sector is education. Education imparts to people the skills and knowledge essential for any form of work. Teachers have a great mission to ignite the minds of the young and make them aware of the possibilities in the world around them. Moreover, as the world becomes increasingly reliant on new technology, lifelong learning will become an integral part of our lives to upgrade our skills as technology expands. Providing such teaching, in itself, is an exciting area of growth.

Education in India

Education needs to perform a multitude of functions in our society:

Teaching a value system: The best part of a person's life is the learning years in school—from five to sixteen. Children need value-based education in school and at home for them to become good citizens. The hours at school are the best time for learning. The child needs the best and most stimulating environment and mission-oriented learning with value system. If the child misses the value-based education of the school campus, no government can establish a society with integrity. If the child misses this period of learning, the nation loses an enlightened citizen.

Causing integration of capacity: We need to give children the capacity for contributing to economic development and nation building. In order to do so, children have to develop three kinds of skills:

- The capacity for research and inquiry: The twenty-first century is about the management of all the knowledge and information that was generated during the preceding centuries. Children must be taught the skills with which they can find a way through the sea of available knowledge, so that they can become the lifelong learners that any sustained economic and political development requires.
- The capacity for creativity and innovation: Creativity has many dimensions—from scientific inventions, discoveries and innovations, to artistic expression. Creative people have the ability to accept change, a willingness to play with ideas and possibilities, flexibility of outlook, and the habit of enjoying the good, while looking for ways to improve it. Creativity involves the willingness to work hard continually to improve ideas and solutions by making alterations and refinements.
- The capacity for entrepreneurial leadership: This involves identifying a problem and then finding its solution in the context of development. Entrepreneurship starts with understanding our needs and wanting to help others as we help ourselves. We need to be willing to undertake new challenges, do things differently and be bold in our thinking.

Removal of social discrimination: The teacher has to play an important role in removing the very concept of discrimination—whether based on race, colour, class, religion, caste, gender or economic disparity—from the minds of children. The best way to do this is by setting an example. If the teacher treats all children in the class as truly equal, regardless of whether the child is a boy or a girl, from a rich or poor family, or whether the child belongs to a particular region or religion, the children will learn to do the same.

> During the last century, the world has undergone a change from agricultural society, where natural labour was the critical factor, to industrial society where the management of technology, capital and labour provided the competitive advantage. In the twenty-first century, a new society is emerging where knowledge is the primary resource instead of capital and labour. Today's education system has to train the knowledge worker of the new millennium.

The Indian school education system

Enrolment in Indian schools has gone up dramatically since Independence.

Primary (Classes I to V)

Year	Boys	Girls
1950–51	60.6%	24.8%
1980–81	95.8%	60.5%
2000–01	100%	85.9%

Upper Primary (Classes VI to X)

Year	Boys	Girls
1950–51	20.6%	4.6%
1980–81	54.3%	28.6%
2000–01	66.7%	49.9%

As you can see, there is a drastic fall in school enrolment as children grow older.

The all-India literacy rate in 2001 was 65.38 per cent. 75.85 per cent of the men were literate, compared to only 54.16 per cent of women. The state with the best literacy rate is Kerala, where 90.92 per cent of the population is literate (94.20 per cent of men, and 89.86 per cent of women). If one state can achieve such figures, then surely all the other states can aspire towards the same.

The Indian higher education system

There has been substantial growth in the higher educational system. India has over 300 universities, and over 3 million people graduate every year. The problem arises after they graduate. Often, the new jobs that are available require specialized training and skills, which a general graduate may not have. As a result, there is an increase in the number of educated but unemployed people year after year.

Another problem is that there are not enough universities which teach subjects which are directly related to job opportunities. When a student finishes school and is about to enter university, he or she is often faced with the option of studying very traditional subjects. Universities need to give students the opportunity to study subjects which are directly related to work opportunities in the market.

The question is: how do we do this?

The educational system should highlight the importance of entrepreneurship. It should help students to acquire the skills that will be useful for them as entrepreneurs. College syllabi for regular arts, science and commerce courses should include topics and practicals in areas where entrepreneurship is possible. Educational institutions should help students to gain an idea of how their education can directly benefit other people and themselves. Students can become involved in knowledge connectivity activities, which would provide them with a vocation and be of assistance to farmers, villagers and entrepreneurs. This is especially true in the case of agricultural universities, which can work with farmers to bring about the Second Green Revolution. Technology-based learning has to become an important curriculum in our schools, colleges and universities.

The Indian Institutes of Technology (IITs) are the biggest and most successful experiments in higher education in the developing world. Bill Gates called the IIT 'an incredible institution that has really changed the world and has the potential to do even more in the years ahead'.

The IITs were the brainchild of Sir Ardeshir Dalal, a technocrat who recognized that technology would have a critical role to play in building a free India. Therefore, it was essential to have engineers of the highest calibre in the country. On his persuasion, Jawaharlal Nehru caused the first IIT to be set up in Kharagpur, West Bengal, in 1951. The first batch of students graduated in 1956. There are now six more IITs: Mumbai (set up in 1958), Chennai (1959), Kanpur (1960), Delhi (1961), Guwahati (1994) and Roorkee (2001).

Since the 1950s, the IITs have been churning out some of the world's best engineers. Today, many of them head the best-known companies in India and all over the world. The institutions are a triumphal testimony to what the Indian higher education system can achieve.

There are also other institutions in India, which have consistently imparted quality education. The two million Indians professionals in the US are from IITs and other such institutions.

Vocational training

Conventional higher education often leads to white-collar jobs. But we have to realize that there is much potential for earning well and positively changing the lives of those around you in other areas as well! There should be options for students who do not want to get a conventional college degree to join vocational education courses, which are more directly related to employment and income generation for students.

Developed countries have much higher availability of vocational courses. For example, if we look at the percentage of vocationally trained people in the labour force in the age group twenty to twenty-four, India clearly needs to focus on this area:

Country	Percentage
India	5.06
Australia	64.11
Korea	95.86
Germany	75.33
UK	68.46

It is a peculiarity of our society, unlike many others, that skills and blue-collar jobs are not regarded as challenging or remunerative, despite our rich tradition in arts, crafts and architecture. We need to systematize the training for these sectors and also give them the respect they deserve. India needs a major 'Skills Mission' to develop this sector. This will only lead to greater economic development for the country.

Distance education

As you know, about 70 per cent of Indians live in villages. It is estimated that a rural population of 700 million people lives in 6 lakh villages. Most universities or colleges are in cities or towns, and it is often not possible for students to travel to cities or towns to study. Distance education is the only method by which we can ensure that quality education is available to every youth in the country.

Apart from providing post-graduate education in remote areas, distance education has to promote widespread literacy, provide skills to the unskilled, and enhance craftsmanship for realizing large value addition in the rural sector. Another essential would be to impart technology-based lessons so that such learning can reach every nook and corner of this country. Only through this can we transform the human resources available in this country into a knowledge society.

There are various distance education programmes available in the country. The Indira Gandhi National Open University was a pioneer in distance education. Course material is sent by post, seminars are held periodically in various centres and there are also programmes on television. The Punjab Technical University also has a successful distance education programme in various professional and technology oriented subjects. A few other universities also have such programmes.

However, India needs more such distance education programmes. These should now take into account the new possibilities opening up due to technological advancements and the improvement in connectivity all over the country. We have all the requisite technology available within the country: fibre optic cables, satellite communication, wireless infrastructure and broadband technology. It is essential that distance education adopts new and up-to-date methods which will make it possible for us to reach the most people in the most effective manner in the shortest possible time.

These are some of the elements which need to be developed in the programmes for distance education in the country:

Virtual classrooms and tele-education: With the growth in information technology, distance education programmes can now have virtual classrooms. The students would not merely be passively listening (as happens with TV education); there would also be scope for interaction and asking question by having two-way connectivity between the teacher and the taught. The best teachers can be taken to the students, irrespective of physical distance. Tele-education has the ability to serve a number of classrooms simultaneously across a region.

e-Learning: The course content can be delivered through the Internet. The material would then be online all the time and freely accessible. It could also be provided on-demand. e-Learning enables the student to become an autonomous learner.

Digital library: Libraries need to be digitized and the books should be available seamlessly across the universities and distance learning programmes for universal access. When a student desires to read a certain book, he or she could be given online access. Tele-education software can be an important tool for the digital library.

One of the major problems India faces is the need to run a vast number of elementary and secondary schools in villages with teachers who love teaching. Therefore, I visualize a scene in which an excellent mathematics teacher teaching in a city classroom can be seen, heard and interacting with the students in small villages in distant parts of the state, or an excellent physics teacher in a village school, whose lessons can reach out to other village and city schools!

The way forward

We should look at the possibility of creating a virtual university in India through networking of all the universities and other educational institutions. This would make it possible for all the networked universities to pool their resources and provide students with a better education than they could manage on their own.

Imagine a scenario where Amartya Sen, the Nobel-Prize-winning economist, is lecturing on economics in Delhi, and you, sitting in your classroom in Chennai, can listen to him live. You can interact with him and ask him questions after the lecture. After the session is over, you can go to your computer and order the books that he mentioned. The books are not in the Madras University library, but it does not matter. Because of the digitized library, you can look up for the book and the text appears on your computer at the touch of a button. Many months later, before an exam, you want to find out exactly what Sen had said. You go to the Madras University, where there are recordings of all lectures, and simply watch it all over again. Does this seem like a dream? It could easily come true.

A virtual university will have the following tasks:

1. Act as a central hub of all universities which are networked.
2. Identify experts of national/international eminence in specialized areas.
3. Coordinate, organize, schedule and broadcast the lecture of specialists at a time convenient to all participants.
4. Record the live transmission of the lecture with interaction details in a databank for easy access by participants for review learning.
5. Digitize all the university libraries and make it available for seamless access by all the universities.
6. Provide for lectures, laboratory learning, and the library, all through the Internet.

This experiment across the country will provide a common platform for schools, colleges, universities and vocational training institutes. This will give equal emphasis on theory and experiments, in spite of the fact that it will be done in the cyberspace. This facility would also help in a huge incentive for the expansion of telecommunication and IT services. All this would lead to bringing together the strengths of different universities to provide the best possible education to Indian students.

In September 2004, the Edusat was launched. This will aid the distance education programmes in the country. The power of the satellite is so great that during a recent visit to South Africa, for the Pan-African Parliament, I offered such a linkage to entire African continent with an Edusat made for Africa by India. Such is the power of technology to reach education to the people.

Healthcare for All

All societies are judged by their ability to provide universal healthcare for the people.

India has an ancient tradition in public healthcare. It was the first country in the world where legislation was enacted to ensure that only licenced doctors could call themselves medical practitioners about 2000 years ago. It was the first country to set up free public hospitals. This was done by Emperor Ashoka (ruled 273 to 232 BCE). He also set up the world's first veterinary hospitals.

Healthcare involves not only the ability to cure diseases, but also to prevent their onset by suitable measures and systems. It also deals with availability of clean drinking water, and good sanitation. Without these two, people fall ill more quickly. Adequate nutrition is another essential aspect of healthcare. Diseases are more likely to affect people who are not in good health due to other reasons and have less resistance to disease.

Among the rich and middle-class families, there is awareness of health-related issues, such as the need for a balanced diet and adequate exercise. There is access to doctors and medical facilities. Among the poor, there may not be awareness of such issues, or the ability to consult doctors. It is such people that the public healthcare system is supposed to aid.

If you have ever been to a government hospital, you will often find that they are very crowded. There are often long queues of very ill people waiting. While many of them have talented doctors, these doctors have too many patients to attend to. Similarly, many government hospitals have fine facilities, but there are too many people using them. As a result, the quality of care that one gets in a government hospital may not always be good.

Requirements for good health:

1. Good sanitary conditions
2. Access to clean drinking water
3. Adequate nutrition, with necessary food supplements
4. Healthy environment at home, school or office, and in factories and mines
5. Preventive healthcare—inoculation, vaccination, immunization and periodic health check-ups

---

The public healthcare system

India has a growing network of primary healthcare centres (PHCs), which are further supplemented by sub-centres and community health centres.

	1985	1996
PHCs	9,118	21,853
Sub-centres	84,053	1,32,778
Community health centres	761	2,420

As you can see from the above table, the number has grown over the last decades, but it is still not enough, given the population of the country. As a result of the paucity of PHCs, often most of these cannot provide tangible healthcare to the vast number of people they are supposed to aid. There are many reasons for this. The supply of medicine can be irregular or limited. There are seldom enough doctors or paramedical staff. There may be government or political interference in its working. As a result, the public healthcare system in India often does not deliver the quality of care it should provide.

Despite all this, India's death rate has come down to 8.49 (per thousand) in 2003 from 14.9 in 1971.

Life expectancy (years)	61.1
Infant mortality rate (per thousand)	68.0
Death rate (per thousand)	8.49
Birth rate (per thousand)	25.8

Sanitation

Did you know? India has the world's most ancient sanitation systems. The first private bathrooms, complete with inlet pipes and drains and flush toilets were found in Mohenjo-Daro. All these date from 3000 BCE. Such bathrooms were found even in humble homes. It is a shame that 5,000 years later, so many homes do not have adequate sanitation, and so many people do not even have access to good public sanitation facilities.

Proper drainage of dirty water, disposal of garbage, sewage and human and industrial wastes are essential for the good health of all those who live and work in the area. If you go to the slums of Delhi or Mumbai, you can see people living in extremely difficult conditions. It is the same in many villages, where water supply is poor and there is often no access to proper toilets.

One organization which works to improve the state of sanitation in the country is Sulabh, founded by Dr Bindeshwar Pathak in 1970. Sulabh is the largest internationally recognized pan-Indian social service outfit with over 35,000 volunteers. It began through Pathak's desire to help scavengers—men and women who carry and dispose of human excreta. He developed a two-pit pour-flush toilet (known as the Sulabh shauchalaya) which did not require scavenging to clean. Subsequently, Sulabh also started pay-and-use public toilets, popularly known as Sulabh Complexes, with bath, laundry and toilet facilities. These are used by about ten million people every day. Sulabh has also pioneered the production of biogas and bio-fertilizer from excreta-based plants.

Drinking water

Despite India being a land of rivers, access to clean, healthy drinking water remains a dream for many people. You must have all seen pictures of women in Rajasthan walking across the desert with pots on their heads to fetch drinking water.

Technology can assist in meeting drinking water needs. A DRDO laboratory in Jodhpur has developed an electro-hydrolysis or desalination process that is used to convert salty, brackish water into potable water. There are many parts of the country where the water is brackish and use of this process can help. Two desalination plants of 20,000 and 40,000 litres have been installed, and as a result, more than 100 villages have water. This can be replicated in different parts of the country.

Control of disease

Some diseases—such as cancer, diabetes, cardiac diseases or genetic disorders—are not really preventable, except perhaps by cultivation of healthy habits. Among communicable diseases, the ones which cause the highest mortality in India are TB, AIDS, and diarrhoea. Earlier, polio used to be a major problem area, but thanks to sustained government campaigns, the disease is now much reduced. You must have seen the Pulse Polio Campaign in the city where you live. Developing an effective vaccine for TB is a priority as existing vaccines are not completely satisfactory.

What is important to remember is that many communicable diseases can be prevented by relatively simple measures:

- Suitable sanitation systems
- Control of disease spreading materials (such as foul water) or vectors (such as mosquitoes)
- Immunization programmes

To let people know how this can be done, health education programmes need to be undertaken. Non-governmental organizations (NGOs) and youth organizations can be recruited for this purpose. Film and television could also be tapped to spread the message. Corporate sponsorship could be secured. We also need to continue the search for inexpensive diagnostic tools and vaccines, so that healthcare can become affordable for all.

How can this be made possible?

It is true that the public health service is under severe strain. However, it is essential to find solutions.

Over the last three decades, there has been increasing commercialization of health services, which in itself is not a bad thing if there is countervailing insurance or social security covers that make them affordable for most. Employers, central, state and local governments should bear the responsibility of assuring people of health security cover.

Corporate hospitals: There has been a substantial growth in corporate hospitals in different cities. These hospitals have been providing quality healthcare to different sections of the society. The healthcare industry has matured and is now equipped with state-of-the-art diagnostics and treatment systems.

If such corporate hospitals could be persuaded to move to rural areas, much of the problem would be solved. However, they will not do so unless there are incentives offered by the government. The government should strive to create joint ventures in healthcare between the public sector and the corporate sector. There have been number of areas in which collaboration has taken place between government departments and private sector institutions. We do not have such collaborations in healthcare, and it is essential that we develop these.

Mobile clinics: In some parts of our country, mobile clinics and research centres are deployed to provide diagnosis and treatment at the doorsteps of rural people. Such facilities, through collaborative efforts of research institutions, medical colleges, government agencies and NGOs, should be increased in number. It is important that these mobile clinics are equipped with the latest equipment for diagnosis and treatment, so that those who cannot reach cities or are unable to afford the treatment in cities are able to avail of the quality of healthcare that is now available in urban India.

In October 2002, a mobile diagnostic centre was launched in Uttaranchal, which embodies the efforts of TIFAC to bring technology closer to the masses. This diagnostic centre has state-of-the-art ultrasound, X-ray and ECG machines, and a computerized pathology laboratory. It also has provisions to provide health education and can maintain computerized medical data for each patient. It is manned by a full team of doctors and technicians and has so far serviced more than 40,000 patients. Such mobile diagnostic centres can go a long way in meeting the needs of India's rural population.

Healthcare as national wealth generator

India has the advantage that while there is availability of world-class diagnostic and treatment systems, the cost for doing so is much less than the same procedures in developed countries. We should take advantage of this and try to attract patients from various countries to India where quality treatment is provided at a relatively low cost.

The healthcare industry must be geared to provide a complete package for patients, which includes diagnostics through telemedicine transportation, stay, hospitalization, treatment and convalescence. India's traditional systems of medicine, such as ayurveda, siddha, unani and others, also attract patients who want holistic alternative therapies. Thus the healthcare industry has the potential to be a national wealth generator.

Complementary medicine

We have seen earlier how India is a storehouse of ancient knowledge about herbs, as well as having abundant supplies of many herbs. This advantage must be integrated with high technology to unlock the tremendous potential in this area.

India has a variety of traditional systems of medicines such as yoga, ayurveda, unani, homeopathy, siddha and naturopathy. These are unique to our country, and are often complementary. It would be ideal if we make such systems a part of the mainstream medical facilities available in hospitals, so that patients can have a choice in determining what kind of treatment they would like to have.

The bringing together of different systems of medicine would also have other advantages. It would enable rapid development of medicines and fast-track clearance of products through integrated clinical trials. This too has the potential to be a great wealth generator for the nation.

The way forward

Our country is rich in human resources. There are many trained and talented scientists, doctors and technologists. The basic infrastructure is available for advanced research and various services. The need of the hour is to network the existing facilities, people and expertise with commitment and conviction to augment the pace of research.

We only have one doctor for every 1,800 people. In some developed countries, the ratio is 1:600. To provide quality healthcare to all our citizens, we need to at least double the number of doctors and paramedic staff in the country. The investment for this need not come from the government alone. Hospitals can also be set up by the private sector if they receive subsidized infrastructural support.

We need to set up 30,000 static telemedicine stations at key locations and provide 20,000 mobile telemedicine units. These will be connected to district and state hospitals and super-speciality hospitals and will bring healthcare closer to every home. This is possible because India has a network of satellite communication.

The Enabling Infrastructure

In order to build a developed India, it is essential not only to have agriculture, manufacturing, strategic industries and services which includes education and healthcare. All these need certain linkages or infrastructure, which enable them to function.

There is no point in higher productivity if the goods produced do not reach the markets in time. The best factories in the world will not work if there is no electricity. Producers in India and buyers around the world will not be able to communicate without telecom facilities. The world today, thanks to the technologies of transportation and telecommunication, has become connected in a much more complex way. Every production centre should have speedy connectivity to the every other part of the country, and indeed the world. Electric power is a facilitating technology for transport and communication.

Instant transfer of information is also essential. We have talked about how it is possible to implement designs created abroad in Indian factories and manufacturing houses, be it for textiles or leather good or engineering. For this we need to have swift information transfer. The whole concept of business process outsourcing (BPO) work depends on such communication. Moreover, it is essential to be able to swiftly transfer information when it comes to credit and money.

The infrastructure consists of:

1. Physical transportation systems: (a) buses, trains, planes, ships; (b) airports, ports, stations; (c) everything which facilitates the transportation: good roads and tracks, efficient checkpoints, if any, good signals and displays.
2. Telecommunications network: telephones, Internet connections, satellites, fibre optic cable networks and mobile telephones.
3. Power, which is crucial for working of both the physical transportation systems as well as the telecommunications network.

If a country's economy is to grow, the government must make sufficient investment in infrastructure. All the above-mentioned linkages must be improved and maintained in top working condition.

The aggregate investment in infrastructure has been growing over the years.

Year	Amount (in Rs crore)
1980–81	6,000
1990–91	29,000
1994–95	50,000

In the Tenth Five Year Plan (2002–07), 26.5 per cent of the total outlay is on energy, 14.8 per cent on transport, and 6.5 per cent on communications. A total of 47.8 per cent of the total outlay is on developing infrastructure in the country. In this chapter, we will look closely at one aspect of infrastructure: power generation.

Power Generation

No nation can aspire to be modern without availability of

quality power for all. The whole magic wand of information technology will come to nothing if there is no electricity. Quality power means stable, uninterrupted supply without variations in voltage or frequency.

Our nation is passing through an energy crisis. There is shortage of power in many parts of the country. Wherever power is available, it is not always reliable. There are many man-hours lost due to unplanned interruptions. One cannot run a modern knowledge economy with such disruptions in communication. There is an immediate need to address the problems and find solutions.

The rapid pace of development in India means that additional quality power is required for commercial as well as non-commercial purposes. As people's standard of living rises, there is additional demand for power for domestic consumption. Over the years, power generation has increased, but so too has demand.

Given below are the actual amounts of electricity generated. This is substantially lower than installed capacity (or the total amount of electricity which could be generated if all plants were working at 100 per cent efficiency).

Power generation	Hydro utilities	Thermal utilities	Nuclear utilities	Non-utilities*	Total
1950–51	2.5	2.6	-	1.5	6.6
1970–71	25.2	28.2	2.4	5.4	61.2
1980–81	46.5	61.3	3.0	8.4	119.3
1990–91	71.7	186.5	6.1	25.1	289.4
2001–02	73.9	422.0	19.3	58.0	573.2

All figures in billion kWh

* Non-utility means power generated for private consumption, such as by a large industry. All the other figures refer to power generated for private consumers and industry.

> **1 kWh** (kilowatt-hour) is the amount of work done by one kilowatt energy acting for one hour. It is the amount of electricity consumed by a 100-watt bulb burning for ten hours.
> **1 MW** (megawatt) is 1,000 watts or 10 kilowatts.

We are now a nation of about 1,070 million people. India's population is expected to rise to 1.5 billion by the year 2050. If we assume that the development aspirations of the people of India would call for per capita electricity generation of about 5,000 kWh per year, the country has to plan to have total electricity generation of about 7,500 billion kWh per year. This is about twelve times the generation in 2001–02. Electricity generation of this magnitude calls for a careful examination of issues such as diversity of energy supply sources and technologies, security of supplies, self-sufficiency, security of energy infrastructure, effect on local, regional and global environments and demand management.

The current power shortages faced by the country has often been cited as one of the main factors hampering industrial growth. The required fossil fuel reserves for power generation are depleting fast. Further, there is a growing concern over the environmental degradation and the warming of the earth, caused by conventional power plants. Against this backdrop, power generation from non-conventional energy resources has assumed significance.

Traditional sources of power

Thermal power: This is the most traditional means of generating electricity, through the burning of fossil fuels such as coal, wood or oil. At present, coal is the mainstay of power generation in India. Today more than 70 per cent of power generation is through the burning of coal.

The quality of coal available in India is poor, with ash content in the range of 35 to 50 per cent. With an estimated coal reserve of 221 billion tons and extremely limited availability of oil and gas, coal will continue to be the mainstay of thermal power generation in India for a long time.

The major disadvantage of thermal power is that coal, oil and wood are all non-renewable resources. Therefore, there will come a day when these are no longer available and other sources of power will have to be found. The dependence on fossil resources, whether coal or oil, has to come down. One initial step would be to use them with better technologies, such as using coal in gasified form.

Using coal for power generation results in the production of about 10,000 million tonnes of fly ash per year. It is important that the fly ash is properly utilized and not dumped. Fly ash can be used to enhance agricultural productivity, and as eco-friendly building material for roads.

Hydroelectric power: This is generated by harnessing the power of water through dams. Falling water, at dams or waterfalls, drives turbines, which in turn drive electricity generators. About 7 per cent of the world's energy is provided by hydroelectricity.

India's first hydroelectric station was constructed in 1897 in Darjeeling.

The oldest of the large power companies in India is Tata Hydro Electric Power Supply Company, established in 1910. J.N. Tata, who also set up India's first large steel company, travelled widely to explore new technologies. After visiting the Niagara Falls to study the hydroelectric generation of power, Jamsetji proposed a hydroelectric scheme with an objective to supply cheap and clean electric power for the growing needs of Mumbai. His dream was fulfilled by his son Dorabji Tata. Tata Electric today is the largest power utility company in the private sector.

The advantage of hydropower is that water is a renewable resource. However, it can cause large-scale displacement of people, which in a country with a high population density is a major issue.

India's rivers are geographically dispersed and in several areas have good potential. Only a part of this potential has been exploited. Some of the biggest hydroelectric power generators are the dams at Damodar Valley, Bhakra Nangal, Hirakud and Nagarjunasagar.

Hydropower, given India's network of rivers, should be tapped to meet the energy demands of small communities through small power projects. Unfortunately, at the present level of technology, networking of rivers still remains very expensive. However, in the long run, it would serve multiple purposes, thereby making the investment feasible.

There are many small or mini hydropower projects in India, which supply electricity for small areas. The advantages of these are that they are relatively cheaper to establish, and also do not cause the problems of displacement of population that larger projects have to contend with.

All issues related to exploitation of this resource need to be addressed and the full hydro-potential needs to be harnessed as far as possible.

Non-conventional energy resources

Solar power: As the name implies, this means energy from the sun. Solar energy is converted into electricity in photovoltaic (solar) cells, which are used to power various devices. You can see this most commonly in calculators which work without cell batteries.

Unlike natural gas, coal, or nuclear power, solar power requires no fuel, works without polluting the air or leaving behind dangerous radioactive waste, and is extremely plentiful. However, it requires an initial investment to convert solar power to electricity or usable energy. Researchers estimate that the sun produces enough energy in a single second to meet the needs of all humanity for 2000 years.

Wind power: Wind turbines generate electricity at wind farms. During the 1980s, more than 20,000 wind turbines were erected around the world. Wind energy today ranks as one of the most promising renewable sources of energy. Scientists estimate that by 2030, wind power could provide more than 10 per cent of the world's electricity.

India is already among the world's five largest producers of wind power with more than 95 per cent of the investment coming from the private sector. There are at present over 200 wind farms in India.

The importance of power generation from wind energy in India was realized during Seventh Five Year Plan (1985–90). India's potential for power generation from wind energy has been assessed as 45,000 MW. The Worldwatch Institute has called India a new 'wind superpower'.

The advantage of wind power is that the cost of establishing wind farms is comparable to that of conventional thermal electricity plants. They are cheap to maintain and pollution-free, and environmentally friendly to a large extent.

Nuclear power: Nuclear energy is generated by the breakdown of uranium and plutonium atoms. There are about 350 nuclear power stations around the world, and they supply more than 5 per cent of the world's electricity. Nuclear power stations do not emit polluting gases or contribute to global warming, but accidents and the disposal of fuel rods pose serious risks.

In India, nuclear power in recent years has been making an increasing contribution to electricity supply and is poised to expand in the years to come. The programme profile spelled out by the DAE envisages the use of domestic uranium resources in Pressurized Heavy Water Reactors, followed by the recycling of spent fuel in Fast Breeder Reactors (FBRs).

Nuclear power is thus a well-established technology in India. Given the uranium and thorium resources of the country, power generation has to take place through the use of FBRs and thorium reactors, which can tap the full energy potential in nuclear fuel materials through the use of recycling technologies.

Thorium is abundant in India. It is necessary to concentrate on technologies to convert thorium to energy, as this is an India-specific strength that we need to be able to utilize.

At present, India has six functioning nuclear power stations:

Nuclear power station	Installed capacity (in MWe*)
Tarapur	320
Rajasthan	740
Kalpakkam	390
Narora	440
Kakrapara	440
Kaiga	440
Total	2770

MWe means megawatts of electrical output

Biomass power: Biomass energy is derived from organic matter such as wood and agricultural waste. Biomass power plants are being built in many countries. They produce little air pollution and do not usually contribute to global warming. Biogas is increasingly also being used to generate power.

Even municipal garbage can be converted into useful

power. There are two plants in Vishakhapatnam and Hyderabad which produce 7.5 MWe with garbage. India needs to have a thousand more such plants.

Biodiesel: It is possible to create biodiesel from plant material, such as the plant *jatropha curcas*, which is found widely in India. This plant has proved to be an excellent energy source.

In 2000, internationally recognized tests established that biodiesel resulted in significant reduction of virtually all regulated emissions, and showed it does not pose a threat to human health. India has made a breakthrough in the production of biodiesel. It is made from domestic surpluses of non-edible vegetable oils, such as ratanjyot, karanj, nagchampa and rubber. It can be manufactured using existing industrial capacity. It can be used with any equipment which uses regular diesel. Even if 8–10 per cent biodiesel is added to diesel, our diesel import would drop, saving vast outflows of foreign exchange.

If biodiesel reaches commercial manufacture on a large scale, it would not only reduce India's substantial fuel import bill, but would also have long-term benefits to the environment.

Power distribution

The rural electrification programme launched in 1951 has succeeded in bringing electricity to more than 5 lakh villages. However, 80,000 villages are yet to get electricity connections. Also, power supply to villages is very intermittent. Quite a few of such villages are in remote areas where conventional electricity grid may not be feasible. Therefore, in rural areas, non-conventional energy sources like generation of power from biomass, wind and solar power can be tried out.

Networking of rivers

The networking of rivers is a vital project to manage the flood–drought conditions that occur repeatedly in some parts of our country. Also, some areas have more potential for hydropower generation. To offset this regional hydro-imbalance, we need to have a water and power mission which will enable widespread availability of water and power without endangering environmental safety. A focus of this project would be to transfer water from areas of surplus to those where there is deficit.

It is our responsibility to ensure that environmental conservation activities become economically profitable. The river networking project should have in its agenda the action plan for increasing the afforestation by certain percentage in the regions of the proposed new canals and storage basins. This project could yield nearly 65,000 MW of power through hydroelectric power generation system.

Environmental pollution from energy use

Energy use is associated with environmental problems. The emissions of sulphur dioxide, nitrogen dioxide and lead from burning fuels cause severe air pollution in urban areas. At the same time, use of dirty biofuels for cooking causes severe indoor air pollution.

So how can one continue to use energy for essential purposes and still not damage the environment? Technologies exist to use energy relatively cleanly so that damage due to air pollution is minimized. This has been done in industrialized countries. For a polluting industry to take care of pollution at source is expensive, but not so expensive that it would put the concern out of business. There needs to be legislation and incentives to do so. If the polluter is asked to bear the cost of health damage he inflicts on others, he will automatically reduce emissions. Society at large would benefit. The higher cost to the energy user would be more than offset by the health benefits gained.

The way forward

There needs to be a three-fold path to solve India's energy problems:

1. Increase investment in conventional power generation routes like thermal electricity and hydroelectricity.
2. Greater emphasis needs to be placed on the generation of power using nuclear energy and renewable energy, such as wind and solar power.
3. Better power distribution and attention to providing quality power and energy conservation measures.

As people now demand clean, renewable energy, there has been a growth in investment in ecologically friendly power such as solar, wind, biomass and small-scale hydroelectric sources of power. Small, commercial solar power plants have begun serving some energy markets. There are many new opportunities for those who are willing to take up the challenge!

Realizing the Vision

Everything is possible. I believe that the creativity of the human mind and the struggles it undergoes to achieve excellence can result in a person doing whatever he or she dreams of. For India to achieve all the goals outlined in this book, and more, all it requires is concerted effort by the people of India, especially the youth who form more than fifty per cent of the population. A major mission-oriented programme needs teamwork, and individuals should be attuned to such functioning.

For a long time, it was commonly believed that human flight was impossible. In 1895, a well-known British scientist, Lord Kelvin, who was the President of Royal Society of London, declared, 'Anything heavier than air cannot fly, and cannot be flown.' Within a decade, the Wright brothers proved man could fly. Several decades later, flying is now a safe and affordable means of transport.

On the successful completion of the first mission to the moon in 1961, Wernher von Braun, the rocket designer who built Saturn-V, which launched the capsule with astronauts and made the moon walk a reality, said, 'If I am authorized, I will remove the word impossible [from the dictionary].' You must also make every difficult task a possible venture.

India: Vision 2020

Can the country be geared up to action to realize the new vision for India 2020? We believe it can. People may ask why we think that there will be action now, when earlier there was a relatively slack period, when development was not that rapid. The answer, we believe, lies in appreciating that a large part of our population is young and raring for change. The missed opportunities are history for them. Also, today there are some inspirational models of 'Made in India' in both the public and private sectors.

The world today is a very different place from what is was. For a start, Indian industry is no longer controlled by the government as it used to be after Independence, when people required licences and permits to launch new ventures. As a result, Indian companies could not compete with the best in the world, and at some level this led to a lack of self-confidence. Today's Indians know that we have launched our own missiles, our IT companies and auto component manufacturers are among the best in the world, and agricultural production is soaring. Our pharmaceutical industries are capturing world markets and are set to invent new drugs. Indian professionals are being recognized for their achievements in all parts of the world. Technology offers many opportunities to unleash people's entrepreneurial spirit, and today many youngsters are prepared to explore new areas of work.

The explosive growth in television, thanks primarily to satellite communications, exposes people to the realities existing elsewhere in the world. 'Why not in India?' is a natural question which arises in the minds of viewers. There are, of course, people who are pessimistic and say that India can't improve because of pervasive corruption, mindless bureaucracy and greedy politicians, but there are also people who want to make things better because the post-liberalization economy has given them the opportunity.

This is what we want, as a nation, to achieve by 2020:

1. India will be a developed nation.
2. India will be one of the five biggest economic powers, having self-reliance in national security, and a standing in world economic and political forums.
3. Agriculture would have become very remunerative to farmers with the success of the Second Green Revolution. India will have surplus food products to export to the world, after domestic consumption is met.
4. Indian agro-processing industries will be among the best in the world.
5. India will capitalize on its vast mineral wealth to emerge as a major techno-industrial global power in various advanced and commercial materials, such as steel and titanium.
6. The Indian chemical industry will be transformed into a technological innovator in clean processes specialty chemicals, pharmaceuticals, biotech and natural products.
7. The Indian manufacturing sector will be a major national and world player in machine tools, foundry and transport equipment. Many engineering products will be designed and made in India. India will be the manufacturing centre of the world.
8. India will emerge as a global leader in the services sector, providing excellent services within the country and outside.
9. In critical elements of the strategic sectors, India will be self-reliant.
10. Through speedy growth of roads, railways, telecommunications and electricity, India will have excellent infrastructure to fulfil the needs of development.
11. Health and education services will reach all people.

How can we realize the vision?
All the things listed above are attainable. However, they will

not happen spontaneously, nor can they be left to the government, planners, scientists or economists alone. Everyone has a role to play, each and every person in India. We should act now, and persevere, regardless of any setbacks we may face along the way.

Below is a list of what different individuals and groups should set themselves as a task:

Youth: In addition to pursuing your studies, think positive about India's future. Spread the news about positive developments in the country among your friends and classmates.

Every person: Devote a few days in a month to doing something better, something speedier, something of high quality, something which will make you proud, something which will make a poorer or suffering person's life a little better.

Academic institutions and R&D labs: You have the unique opportunity to be a front runner. Each lab or institution should launch a project on its own, in addition to contributing to their respective ministries or Public Sector Units (PSUs). You will find financial contributions if you look around your own area.

NGOs: Your role is as multifarious and as complex as India. Try to help in creating a climate for positive actions and rapid change for the better.

Media: Spread the message of success, however small the successes are. There are many grim events and developments that you can cover, but the positive developments also have to be news. Build up an image of India with hundreds and thousands of heroes and heroines who are changing the country's destiny.

Central PSUs must undertake one project each to make a developed India. Unleash your technological strengths. This is in addition to the missions your ministry may launch and to which you will contribute. The key is to create initiative at the unit level by the leaders and staff of PSU.

State PSUs: In at least one area, transform yourself to service the people in your area. If possible, launch one project with partners on similar lines that goes beyond your region.

Government departments (Central and state) must undertake one mission each to realize the vision of a developed India, preferably in partnership with other departments, NGOs, agencies and the private sector. Don't wait to start! Others will join you, if you start well!

Large industries (private sector): Each industry should launch a project similar to what is suggested for PSUs, in addition to its own corporate plans and other demands placed on it by government-sponsored projects. Also create projects to uplift small-scale industries or agriculture technologically. Such projects should have commercial viability, *not* depend on subsidies.

Small industries: Even though your problems may be many, look ahead. Learn to capture a few technological strengths. Work with a nearby academic institution or laboratory. You will find some people there with innovative fire. Once you find a knowledge source relevant to your business, life will be transformed for you.

MNCs: In addition to your profits and global strategies, look at the one-billion-plus country with inherent strengths as a partner and not as a short-term market. Demonstrate clearly through one or two projects each that you want to create core competitive strengths in India, to help it march towards a developed status.

People of Indian Origin (PIO)/Non-Resident Indians (NRIs): You can inspire other Indians and also bring global networks for Indian products and services.

Other global India lovers: You can make 'India Brand' spread globally.

Integrated action

India has about 260 million people living below the poverty line. The nation has to ensure that they earn more and can live a good life. The GDP growth rate has to be raised to 10 per cent and has to be sustained at this level for several years. Only then will it be possible for India to develop economically and the billion people will actually feel the prosperity of the nation. The road map involves integrated action in the following five areas:

1. **Agriculture and food processing**: We have to produce 360 million tons of food and agricultural products. Other areas of agriculture—such as milk, poultry, animals, horticulture, floriculture, herbs—and food processing have to be developed to bring prosperity to rural people and speed up economic growth.
2. Reliable and quality **infrastructure**, including **electricity**, for all parts of the country.
3. **Education and healthcare**, of good quality, need to be available to every citizen, regardless of where he or she lives.
4. **Information communication technology** is one of our core competencies, and can be used to promote education in remote areas and to create national wealth.
5. **Strategic sectors** have witnessed growth in nuclear, space and defence technology, and this growth needs to be sustained.

What can *you* do?

For a start, it is important that you be aware of the vision and of all the factors that will help in making it come true. When you make your decisions about what you want to do with your life, what you want to study, what work you want to do, be aware of how all this can contribute to the vision.

You can also tell others about this vision, and make your family and friends share it and do their bit to help realize it. Collect and share positive stories of how people are working towards this vision.

There are four specific ways in which I believe every student can contribute to the realization of Vision 2020:

1. **Be industrious**: We must work together with great determination and effort. By sheer resolution, much can be achieved. Look at the miracles that were achieved by Japan and Germany after World War II. You too must work hard at whatever you are doing.

2. **Be inventive**: We have seen the way that the Indian IT industry has grown from virtually nothing to an industry which is winning India much global recognition. This industry has largely grown on its own, without too much government assistance. You too can think creatively to find a niche of opportunity in which you think you can help India develop.

3. **Learn governance**: No development is possible unless there is a stable framework of government, which helps individuals. It is important that governments are responsive to the needs of people and at the same time help to regulate them. You too can practise this at your school, by participating in student government. You can help formulate policies for students and organize events. Learn to facilitate without attempting to control. This is all good practice, if some day you too decide to be part of the governance of India. Even if you do not, it is always good practice for whatever work you do in life, and for learning how to work with people.

4. **Do your civic duty**: Participate, enthusiastically and creatively, in civic programmes in your school and neighbourhood—whether it is cleaning up a local park,

planting trees, helping underprivileged children, or even keeping your school campus clean. This can transform not only your immediate environment, but also India as a whole. Look at the transformation that has happened in Singapore, once an untidy city. Today, due to programmes started by the government and willingly assisted by its citizens, Singapore has become one of the cleanest cities in the world. If each student worked towards the cleaning of their own neighbourhood, the polluted urban centres of India could become clean and beautiful.

The ten-point oath

This is an oath that I believe every child in our country should live up to. Read it carefully. If you can make it a point to do these ten things, then you will have started to do your bit to realize the vision of India 2020.

1. I will pursue my education or the work with dedication and I will excel in it.
2. I will teach at least ten persons who cannot read or write to do so.
3. I will plant at least ten saplings and ensure their growth through constant care.
4. I will visit rural and urban areas and work hard to permanently wean away at least five persons from addiction and gambling.
5. I will constantly endeavour to remove the pain of my suffering brethren.
6. I will not support any religious, caste or language differentiation.
7. I will be honest and set an example for others to follow.
8. I will work towards becoming an enlightened citizen and make my family righteous. I will respect all women and

support women's education.

9. I will always be a friend of the mentally and physically challenged, and will work hard to make them feel like the rest of us.

10. I will proudly celebrate the success of my country and my people.

The youth of India should have an indomitable spirit. This means two things: firstly, you should have an aim and work for it; and secondly, if you encounter some problems while doing so, do not allow them to become your master. Become master of the problems; defeat them and succeed.

One of our nation's greatest assets is the young people in it. The ignited minds of the young are the greatest resource on earth, under earth and above earth. When ignited minds work with indomitable spirit, a prosperous, happy and safe India is assured.

I wish you all success.

Acknowledgements

In writing *India 2020: A Vision for the New Millennium*, upon which *Mission India: A Vision for Indian Youth* is based, our ideas were shaped by several hundred Indians—some very well known. Each interaction enriched our experience and added a new dimension to our understanding of India's developmental needs and actions required. It is difficult to list every name. First and foremost, we are thankful to the chairpersons and co-chairpersons of the various Technology Vision task forces and panels as well as the coordinators and the key TIFAC persons who helped in the whole Vision 2020 exercise. In addition, there was the encouragement and the help of the members of the Governing Council of TIFAC. We thank Professor V.S. Ramamurthy, Secretary, Department of Science and Technology, for the encouragement and the permission given to use materials from TIFAC reports.

Integral to the writing of the book was the tireless effort of H. Sheridon. Krishan Chopra of Penguin Books provided excellent project management in shaping the book. Sayoni Basu has adapted the earlier version with great skill and J.R. Krishnan has coordinated the entire effort, and we are thankful to both.

Y.S. Rajan would like to thank his wife Gomati, who has been a great source of strength, and his son Dr Vikram Rajan for their support.

A.P.J. Abdul Kalam would like to place on record his thanks to the thousands of Indians who write to him on several occasions and inspire him to undertake several technological tasks for India.